MW01146403

1 CORINTHIANS
One in Christ

The message of the cross is foolishness to those who are perishing,
but to us who are being saved it is the power of God.

1 Corinthians 1:18

Compiled and edited by Lois M. Engfehr

CONCORDIA PUBLISHING HOUSE · SAINT LOUIS

Series editors: Thomas J. Doyle and Rodney L. Rathmann

Scripture taken from the HOLY BIBLE, NEW INTERNATIONAL VERSION®. NIV®. Copyright © 1973, 1978, 1984 by International Bible Society. Used by permission of Zondervan Publishing House. All rights reserved.
Manufactured in the United States of America

We solicit your comments and suggestions concerning this material. Please write to Product Manager, Adult Bible Studies, Concordia Publishing House, 3558 S. Jefferson Avenue, St. Louis, MO 63118-3968.

Manufactured in the United States of America

3   4   5   6   7   8   9   10   11   12   13   12   11   10   09   08   07   06   05   04

Contents

Introduction

While studying 1 Corinthians, remember that it is not a formal doctrinal essay. It is a letter. Although divinely inspired, it is a personal document written by a real person to real people. It is practical, presenting everyday problems confronting Christians in the world. It is helpful, supplying God's answers to daily problems.

So you are opening a letter. The next thing to do is to read it. Read it through as you would any other letter. You can come back to particular paragraphs later.

The original readers of the letter were members of the "church of God" at Corinth. The founding of this congregation is reported in **Acts 18.** Read also **Acts 16:6–10, 17.**

Corinth was a Greek seaport with a waterfront, traffic, travelers, sailors, and merchants. It was cosmopolitan, pagan, idolatrous, immoral, wide-open, tough. Corinth was the fourth-largest city in the Roman Empire. Among its inhabitants were Roman colonists, ex-slaves, former soldiers, admirers of Greek wisdom and culture, and a scattering of Jews. It was a very prosperous and wealthy but irreligious city.

When Christianity collided with paganism in Corinth, the young congregation there was naturally plagued with many problems and questions. Some of these related to congregational factions, lawsuits, promiscuity, marriage and divorce, desertion, the place of women in the church, Holy Communion, and the resurrection of the body. The Corinthians turned to Paul for guidance and counsel. His letter contains God's answers and counsel.

The church at Corinth was not a perfect congregation. But Paul's letter to the church at Rome also shows how the grace of God in Christ makes up for that. "Where sin increased, grace increased all the more" **(Romans 5:20).**

The experiences of the Corinthians are increasingly those of present-day Christians, not only in traditionally heathen countries but also in so-called Christian lands slipping deeper into pagan ways. The impact of the world's morals and mores on church people is evident today, with political factions growing, marriages failing, sexual morality sinking, and church disorders increasing. The Christian today faces many of the moral dilemmas reflected in this epistle.

At the same time, 1 Corinthians is a document of hope for our times. In trying to hold the Corinthians to the Word of God, Paul found it necessary to state both their human faults and their proper goals. In his epistle, Paul shows them the way of error and the way of truth in an alternating pattern.

Lesson 1

The Power of Forgiveness (1 Corinthians 1:1–31)

Theme Verse

"The foolishness of God is wiser than man's wisdom, and the weakness of God is stronger than man's strength" **(1 Corinthians 1:25).**

Goal

Although all Christians are imperfect, God—through the Gospel—gives us forgiveness and the power for improvement.

What's Going On Here?

1 Corinthians is part of an extended correspondence between Paul and the Christians at Corinth. From this letter we see a good picture of Paul as a pastor, interpreting and applying the Gospel to the problems of this congregation. After his greeting, the apostle Paul expresses thanksgiving to God for the spiritual sufficiency of the Corinthian flock in the fellowship of the Gospel. He immediately takes up the reported dissensions, dwelling on them to the end of **chapter 4.** Paul stresses that through the Word of the cross, God has acted to bring people to salvation. Since God has accomplished this also among the Corinthians, the Gospel of Christ is far superior to human wisdom and power, and in all humility, humankind must glorify God for His work.

Searching the Scriptures

Read all of **1 Corinthians 1.** Paul wrote this open letter to the congregation at Corinth in approximately A.D. 55. He used the letter format of the day, identifying himself at the beginning as the author, indicating to whom he addressed the letter, and giving a word of greeting.

Paul's Greeting (1 Corinthians 1:1–3)

1. Note the credentials Paul presents in **verse 1.** How would mentioning these credentials be important to his task?

2. Paul describes the church in Corinth as "sanctified ... and called to be holy." "Sanctified" means to be set apart for God's purposes; "holy" means to be separated from sin and consecrated to God. Read **John 17:17, 19** and **1 Thessalonians 5:23–24.** What do you learn from these passages about how you are sanctified and become holy?

3. Why was **1 Corinthians** written? What do the following passages reveal about how Paul learned about some of the problems in the church at Corinth?

a. **1 Corinthians 1:11**

b. **1 Corinthians 7:1a**

c. **1 Corinthians 16:17**

Paul's Thanksgiving (1 Corinthians 1:4–17)

1. Paul writes that he "always" (**v. 4**) thanks God for the congregation at Corinth. For what specific things does he thank God in **verses 4, 5, 6, and 7?**

2. How does Paul encourage the Corinthian Christians in **verse 8?**

3. What was the quarrel about in the Corinthian church?

Start
here

The Cross, God's Way of Salvation (1 Corinthians 1:18–25)

1. In **verse 18,** Paul refers to the "message of the cross," which he identifies as "the power of God." Why do we need saving? (Read **Romans 3:10–12, 23** and **6:23a.**)

2. How did God save us? (Read **John 19:18** and **Colossians 1:19–20.**)

3. Why was it necessary for Jesus to suffer a cruel death on the cross to accomplish our salvation? (Read **Hebrews 9:22** and **2 Corinthians 5:18–19, 21.**)

God's Action in Corinth (1 Corinthians 1:26–31)

1. The Corinthians were not "wise by human standards" **(v. 26)**, nor were they influential or of noble birth. But God chose them and called them to faith. Why did God choose to call ordinary people rather than those who might more easily impress the world?

2. Consider what Paul says about this in **1:28–29** and **2:5.** Try to put what you learn from these verses into your own words.

3. As you read what the Corinthians were and were not **(vv. 27–28)** as far as this world is concerned, how would you say this compares with the situation today? Does the Christian Gospel seem to appeal today especially to one class of people as compared to other classes of people?

The Word for Us

1. Paul wrote this letter to help the church deal with problems such as divisions, immorality, and lawsuits. He also wanted to correct abuses connected with speaking in tongues and the Lord's Supper. He wrote to correct false teachings about the resurrection. Finally, he wanted to give instruction about the collection for the poor in Jerusalem. In addressing these serious issues, Paul wrote with a spirit of humility and dependence upon the Holy Spirit for guidance. How would such a spirit be important also in approaching problems that affect our churches today?

2. For what specific things can you thank God regarding your own congregation?

3. Factions in the Corinthian church identified themselves with certain leaders: Paul, Apollos, Cephas, and Christ (v. 12). What problems do you think such personality cliques would cause in a congregation?

4. In saying that he baptized few people, Paul is not dismissing or denying the importance of Baptism. Paul speaks of Baptism in lofty terms in other passages (e.g., **Romans 6:4** and **Galatians 3:27**). Paul is merely making a distinction between the task he was called to do and the task others were called to do. This distinction might be made by the terms "evangelism" and "nurture."

a. How would you distinguish between "evangelism" and "nurture"?

b. How are you personally involved in each of these two critical areas of your congregation's ministry (e.g., praying for evangelism callers, teaching Sunday school)?

5. Paul distinguishes between the human and the divine in the task of presenting the Gospel **(vv. 18–25).** What reassurance does this passage offer to someone who attempts to present the Gospel to another person?

Closing

Sing or speak together these stanzas of "Salvation unto Us Has Come":

Salvation unto us has come
By God's free grace and favor;
Good works cannot avert our doom,
They help and save us never.
Faith looks to Jesus Christ alone,
Who did for all the world atone;
He is our one redeemer.

Since Christ has full atonement made
And brought to us salvation,
Each Christian therefore may be glad
And build on this foundation.
Your grace alone, dear Lord, I plead,
Your death is now my life indeed,
For You have paid my ransom.

Lesson 2

Wisdom from the Holy Spirit (1 Corinthians 2:1–16)

Theme Verses

"My message and my preaching were not with wise and persuasive words, but with a demonstration of the Spirit's power, so that your faith might not rest on men's wisdom, but on God's power" (**1 Corinthians 2:4–5**).

Goal

In this lesson we will see how the message of the cross is the message of God's love and all that it does for us. Apart from Christ there is no way of knowing that the Creator and Controller of our world loves us as much as He does and forgives our sins. That great demonstration of God's love can register only as the Holy Spirit enlightens our minds and impresses it upon our hearts.

What's Going On Here?

Paul had intentionally proclaimed the message of Jesus Christ and Him crucified in plain terms so that the Corinthians' faith might not rest in human rhetoric and wisdom but in the work of God. In declaring the uniqueness of the Gospel, the apostle finds its source in the depth of divine wisdom and its meaning revealed only by the Holy Spirit. As little as humankind could have invented the Gospel, so little can humankind understand it by the powers of the natural mind. In contrast, Christians can discern and judge the revealed truth because the Holy Spirit has given them the "mind of Christ" (**v. 16b**).

Searching the Scriptures

Read aloud or summarize **1 Corinthians 2:1–16.**

Paul's Message of the Cross (1 Corinthians 2:1–5)

1. Paul has often been called one of Christianity's most important preachers and evangelists because of the great missionary work he did. What was Paul's own assessment of his preaching skills **(vv. 3–4)?**

2. Nevertheless, Paul's preaching was effective. How does Paul account for the effectiveness of his preaching in **verses 2** and **4?**

God, the Author of the Gospel (1 Corinthians 2:6–16)

1. Paul describes God's wisdom as "secret" and "hidden" **(v. 7).** He means that human wisdom by itself could never have figured out God's thinking. In **verse 8,** Paul points to the crucifixion of Jesus as proof of this. How would you say that the crucifixion of Jesus shows the failure of human thinking to understand God's plan?

2. Just as the words that Paul preached and wrote were taught to him by the Spirit **(2:13),** so Paul says that no person can understand this Spirit-taught message unless the Spirit also enables that person to understand. Why can't people come to faith or remain in faith without the work of the Holy Spirit? How do the following passages explain this?

a. **1 Corinthians 2:14**

b. **Ephesians 2:1–5**

c. **Romans 8:6–8**

The Word for Us

1. What lesson(s) do you think Christians today might draw from what Paul says about his own sharing of the Gospel?

2. Paul discusses the wisdom that comes from God (as distinct from the wisdom that comes from human thinking, **v. 5**). He begins by saying that God's wisdom is for the mature. What would you say are some characteristics of a mature Christian?

3. In **1 Corinthians 1:24,** Paul refers to Jesus as "Christ the power of God and the wisdom of God." How has your relationship with Christ enabled you to experience the "power of God" and the "wisdom of God"?

Closing

Sing or speak together these stanzas of "You Are the Way; to You Alone":

> You are the way; to You alone
> From sin and death we flee;
> And He who would the Father seek
> Your follower must be.
>
> You are the truth; Your Word alone
> True wisdom can impart;
> You only can inform the mind
> And purify the heart.

Lesson 3

Jesus Christ, the Sure Foundation (1 Corinthians 3:1–23)

Theme Verse

"No one can lay any foundation other than the one already laid, which is Jesus Christ" (**1 Corinthians 3:11**).

Goal

In this lesson we will see how Jesus is the foundation of our Lord's church. He lives in the heart of each believer, and when we gather together in His name, He promises to be right there with us.

What's Going On Here?

The Corinthians had shown spiritual immaturity ("mere infants in Christ") in wanting to follow human leaders, whether Paul, Cephas (Peter), or Apollos. The apostle reminds emphatically that it is not man but God who is the true tiller of spiritual soil and builder of His church. It is important, then, that workers in God's employ build up the Christian congregation, or the temple of God, on the basis of the Word of God. Those who construct the church on the sure foundation of the Gospel of Christ will see their work survive. But those who build otherwise interfere with the orderly growth of the church and bring themselves and their work under divine judgment. It is both futile and foolish, as well as contrary to its duties and rights, for a Christian congregation to subject itself to the opinions of human leaders who depart from the Word of God.

Searching the Scriptures

Read aloud or summarize **1 Corinthians 3:1–23.**

Christian Immaturity (1 Corinthians 3:1–4)

1. In **1 Corinthians 3:1,** Paul picks up the concept of "mature" from **1 Corinthians 2:6** but here uses the term "spiritual" and contrasts it with "worldly." Read **verses 1–2** and **Hebrews 5:11–14.** Explain what you understand these passages to mean by *milk* and *solid food.*

2. It is the spiritual age of the Corinthians of which Paul writes. Read **Acts 20:32** and **Ephesians 4:11–16** and summarize what these passages say about how Christians mature.

"You Are God's Field" (1 Corinthians 3:5–9)

1. Paul calls himself and Apollos "servants" to whom God has assigned specific tasks **(3:5–8; 4:1).** What tasks had God entrusted to Paul and Apollos regarding the church at Corinth?

2. While their tasks differed, Paul and Apollos served one purpose **(v. 8).** What was that purpose **(3:5)?**

3. Paul refers to a reward God will give to all His faithful servants who go about their several tasks **(3:8)**. How does the master reward his faithful servants in Jesus' parable recorded in **Matthew 25:19–23?**

Jesus Christ, the Foundation
(1 Corinthians 3:10–15)

Paul refers to the church by using several descriptive terms: God's field **(vv. 6–9)**; God's building **(vv. 9–13)**; and God's temple **(vv. 16–17)**. The first step in the construction of the building is laying the foundation. Paul identifies Jesus Christ as the foundation upon which the building rests **(v. 11)**.

1. Read **Matthew 7:24–27**. In what way(s) does Jesus provide a solid foundation?

2. Paul declares that he laid that foundation in Corinth. Reread **1 Corinthians 2:2** to see how he did that. What do you conclude about Paul's view of himself as a church builder from the phrases "by the grace God has given me" and "as an expert builder" **(v. 10)?**

3. In **verses 12–15,** Paul contrasts building materials that will endure (gold, silver, costly stones) to those that will not endure (wood, hay, straw). The quality of workmanship will be made evident when the Lord returns **(v. 13)**. How might churches be tempted to build using other building materials than the Gospel of Jesus Christ?

You Are God's Temple (1 Corinthians 3:16–23)

1. The third word picture Paul uses is that of a temple **(vv. 16–17)**. Paul refers here not to Christians as individuals but to the whole church as the body of believers. Just as the Holy Spirit dwells within each individual Christian **(6:19)**, the Holy Spirit dwells within the church as a body of believers. How can viewing the church as the dwelling of the Holy Spirit, as sacred and as under God's watchful protection, encourage us when we are disappointed in the failings or weaknesses of other church members?

2. What is the solution for divisions in the church **(vv. 21–23)**?

The Word for Us

1. Reflect on your own spiritual growth. In what areas do you need most to grow through a more intensive use of the Word in your daily life? In what areas do you feel you have grown the most? How can you grow spiritually **(Acts 20:32; Ephesians 4:1–5, 14–15)**?

2. Consider your own role in God's kingdom. What specific tasks has God assigned to you? How can you be sure your work for the Lord is not just wasted time?

3. Examine your own priorities in life. How are you spending your time, talents, and treasure in ways that will endure beyond this life into heaven? Are any changes of priorities in order? Explain.

Closing

Sing or speak together these stanzas of "The Church's One Foundation":

The Church's one foundation
Is Jesus Christ, her Lord;
She is His new creation
By water and the Word.
From heav'n He came and sought her
To be His holy bride;
With His own blood He bought her,
And for her life He died.

Elect from ev'ry nation,
Yet one o'er all the earth;
Her charter of salvation:
One Lord, one faith, one birth.
One holy name she blesses,
Partakes one holy food,
And to one hope she presses
With ev'ry grace endued.

Lesson 4

Spiritual Leadership (1 Corinthians 4:1–21)

Theme Verse

"So then, men ought to regard us as servants of Christ and as those entrusted with the secret things of God" **(1 Corinthians 4:1).**

Goal

As servants of Christ through whom people come to faith and grow in faith, pastoral leaders are to be appreciated and respected, but they are not to be made the center of Christian loyalty.

What's Going On Here?

With **chapter 4** Paul concludes his counsel to the factions in the Corinthian congregation. In this chapter he refers to himself and Apollos as servants and stewards who are accountable only to God. To the Corinthians, who in pride had set themselves up as critics of one another and of God's servants in their midst, such faithfulness and humility may well serve as an example. In relation to his Lord, Paul thinks of himself as a steward subject only to God's judgment. In relation to the Christians in Corinth, he is as a father to children. Whether he is present or absent, whether he speaks words of correction or of comfort, he always has their spiritual welfare at heart.

Searching the Scriptures

Read aloud or summarize **1 Corinthians 4:1–21.**

Servants and Stewards (1 Corinthians 4:1–7)

1. The term "servant" Paul uses originally referred to a slave who served as a house manager or steward of his owner's possessions. In **1 Corinthians 4:1,** Paul says he and his co-workers are entrusted with "the secret things of God." The word *secret* is often translated as *mystery*, referring to something that can be known only when God reveals it. How does God reveal His mysteries to us? (See **Romans 16:25–27; 1 Corinthians 2:12–13.**)

2a. To what standard of faithfulness can a congregation rightly hold the pastor accountable **(Acts 17:11)?**

b. To what standard of faithfulness can the community in which the pastor lives hold him accountable **(1 Timothy 3:7)?**

c. To what standard of faithfulness can he hold himself accountable **(1 Timothy 3:9)?**

d. To what standard of faithfulness does the Lord hold him accountable **(1 Corinthians 4:2–5)?**

Proud Critics but Humble Apostles
(1 Corinthians 4:8–13)

1. Paul uses irony and sarcasm to try to get the Corinthians to see their pride, haughtiness, and spiritual immaturity. What do you think Paul means in **verse 8** when he writes that, in their own estimation, they had "become kings"?

2. What hardships and persecutions did Paul endure for the sake of Christ **(2 Corinthians 11:23–29)?**

3. What does Paul say that such experiences revealed about himself in **2 Corinthians 11:30; 12:5, 9–10?**

Fatherly Admonitions (1 Corinthians 4:14–21)

1. Paul refers to himself as the spiritual father of the Corinthians since he had first brought the Gospel to Corinth. In what ways does Paul offer himself as an example in **1 Corinthians 4:17** and **1 Corinthians 10:31–11:1?**

2. In another father-child reference, Paul calls his co-worker Timothy "my son" **(v. 17).** Read **Acts 16:1–3** and **1 Timothy 1:2a.** In what sense was Timothy Paul's son?

3. What understanding is behind the expression "if the Lord is willing" **(1 Corinthians 4:19)?** (See **James 4:13–15.**)

The Word for Us

1. Paul says the primary requirement of a servant or steward is faithfulness to his duty **(v. 2).** In his letters to his young co-worker Timothy, Paul writes about the duties of a minister. Read **1 Timothy 4:11–16.** How do these duties apply to ministers of churches today?

2. Do you know of anyone who is being persecuted in any way or who is suffering hardship because of their faithfulness to Christ? If so, what could you do to help or encourage them?

3. When the apostles were persecuted, they responded as Christ commanded **(Matthew 5:11–12, 44).** Is there any way in which you might have the opportunity to practice Christ's command in your own life? If so, share your thoughts with your discussion group.

4. Note how Paul speaks to some in the congregation at Corinth in **1 Corinthians 4:18–21.** The arrogance of some in the congregation could only be met with a rebuke if their attitude did not change. While Christians prefer to deal with one another with gentleness, sternness is sometimes required. Explain why this is so.

Closing

Sing or speak together these stanzas of "Speak, O Lord, Your Servant Listens":

Speak, O Lord, Your servant listens,
Let Your Word to me come near;
Newborn life and spirit give me,
Let each promise still my fear.
Death's dread pow'r, its inward strife,
Wars against Your Word of life;
Fill me, Lord, with love's strong fervor
That I cling to You forever!

Lord, Your words are waters living,
When my thirsting spirit pleads;
Lord, Your words are bread life-giving,
On Your words my spirit feeds.
Lord, Your words will be my light
Through death's vale, its dreary night;
Yes, they are my sword prevailing,
And my cup of joy unfailing!

Lesson 5

Potential for Regression (1 Corinthians 5:1–13)

Theme Verse

"Get rid of the old yeast. … For Christ, our Passover lamb, has been sacrificed" (**1 Corinthians 5:7**).

Goal

Even strong and spiritually gifted Christians are capable of serious moral regression, and when this occurs they must be dealt with appropriately. How thankful we can be that the Spirit is available and His power is effective as He works in us through His Word and sacraments.

What's Going On Here?

Having sought to unify the Corinthian church (**chapters 1–4**), Paul next turns his attention to problems of immorality (**chapters 5–6**). He takes up the case of a church member who lived with his father's wife, calling it an instance of morality that even pagan society did not sanction. Disciplinary action was made difficult because others defiantly and arrogantly took the sinner's part. The apostle urges that the evil leaven be purged, lest it permeate the entire congregation. He wants the members to be under the sincere and truthful power of Christ as Paschal Lamb offered for the church's renewal. As for associations with immoral persons in the world, Paul concedes that not all such contacts can be avoided. However, fellowship with such people is to be shunned.

Searching the Scriptures

Read aloud or summarize **1 Corinthians 5:1–13.**

A Grave Public Scandal (1 Corinthians 5:1–5)

1. The "sexual immorality" that the congregation permitted in the life of one of its members—behavior not even acceptable in pagan society—was that a man "had his father's wife." Some Bible scholars suggest that, since Paul does not say "his mother," the woman was the man's stepmother. Read **Leviticus 18:8** and **17.** These verses refer to the same sin. How does Leviticus characterize incestuous adultery? Explain.

2. Note the penalty for this sin prescribed in **Leviticus 18:29** and **Deuteronomy 27:20.** Compare that penalty with the action prescribed by Paul in **1 Corinthians 5:4–5, 13.** Explain why the drastic action Paul commands is appropriate.

The Lesson of the Leaven (1 Corinthians 5:6–13)

1. Paul compares the presence of the man persisting in unrepentant sin to yeast that must be thrown out so that it does not work its way through an entire batch of dough **(vv. 6–7).** Yeast (or leaven) here is symbolic of sin. This illustration refers to the practice commanded by God in the Old Testament of sweeping the leavened bread crumbs out of the house before preparing the Passover meal, which included unleavened (yeast-free) bread. Try to describe how tolerating sinful behavior within a group can work like yeast in a batch of dough.

2. The highlight of the Old Testament Passover observance came when families ate the Passover lamb together. Why do you think Paul called Christ our Passover Lamb in **1 Corinthians 5:7?** (Read **Exodus 12:21–23** and **John 1:29.**)

3. In the last part of this chapter, Paul writes about judging others. Note the distinction Paul makes in **verses 12–13.** He says we are not to be concerned about judging unbelievers, for God will judge them. Rather than concerning ourselves with judging the behavior of unbelievers, we are to focus on the behavior of believers. The purpose of judging those inside the church is not to condemn but to restore them. Read **Galatians 6:1–5.** What spirit or attitude do you find in that passage?

The Word for Us

1. The decision to exclude a persisting, unrepentant sinner is not to be made by individuals but by the congregation as a whole. Refer to **Matthew 18:20** and **1 Corinthians 5:4.** How would knowing that Jesus is present influence a congregation dealing with this type of situation? (Read **John 3:16–17.**)

2. In **verses 9–11,** Paul writes about the associations we make with others. While we cannot avoid associating with unbelievers as long as we live in this world, Paul writes that we are not to associate with those who call themselves Christians but whose behavior openly dishonors Christ. What do you think Paul is concerned about?

3. In the last part of this chapter Paul writes about judging others. Note the distinction Paul makes in **verses 12–13.** He says we are not to be concerned about judging unbelievers, for God will judge them. Rather than concerning ourselves with judging the behavior of unbelievers, we are to focus on the behavior of believers. Jesus speaks about where this judging is to begin in **Matthew 7:1–5.** State briefly in your own words where we are to begin in judging those inside the church.

Closing

Pray together, **Thank You, Jesus, our Savior, for being the center of our lives. Thank You for curing the terminal sin that infects us and granting us new life now and forever with You. Through Your Word and sacraments keep us in that faith always. In Your name we pray. Amen.**

Lesson 6

Moral Regression (1 Corinthians 6:1–20)

Theme Verse

"You were bought at a price. Therefore honor God with your body" **(1 Corinthians 6:20).**

Goal

In this lesson we will see how our regression may not take the same forms as it did among the Corinthians, but our weaknesses and failings are similar enough to make us stop and think. How thankful we can be that God has provided a Savior!

What's Going On Here?

Continuing his discussion of Christian morality in an immoral society, Paul speaks first of the Corinthians' readiness to take one another to court. Instead of settling differences among themselves, brother went to law against brother before unbelieving judges. This, Paul contends, is inconsistent with the high status of Christians. Underlying these practices is the failure of the Corinthians to realize that as people set apart by saving faith, they can no longer make common cause with any form of pagan immorality. Proceeding to sins of the body, Paul condemns sexual promiscuity because it profanes the body, which the Holy Spirit has honored as His sanctuary. As people wholly redeemed by Christ, let Christians glorify God also in their bodies.

Searching the Scriptures

Read aloud or summarize **1 Corinthians 6:1–20.**

Christians Going to Court (1 Corinthians 6:1–8)

1. Paul moves on to another problem in the Corinthian congregation, that of Christians going to a pagan court to settle matters among themselves. Read **Romans 13:3–5.** Restate, in your own words, what this passage teaches about the primary function of government.

2. Paul argues that Christians can settle their own affairs since they will one day judge the world **(Matthew 19:28** and **Revelation 20:4a).** He also says that the saints will judge angels **(v. 3).** Since the holy angels are unable to sin, to whom is Paul referring **(Revelation 12:7–9)?**

3. Paul speaks directly to the Christian who believes that he or she has been wronged by another Christian. Reread **verses 7–8** and restate in your own words the solution Paul proposes.

Out of the Mire of Pagan Vices (1 Corinthians 6:9–11)

1. Note the kinds of "wicked" people Paul lists in **verses 9–10.** A similar list of wickedness is found in **Galatians 5:19–21.** Compare the two lists to arrive at a composite list.

2. The Lord forbids homosexual sins together with other sexual sins in **Leviticus 18** (note **verse 22**). **Leviticus 20** prescribes the death penalty for some specific sexual sins. How could it be said that this death penalty for sin is still in force **(Romans 6:23)?**

3. What good news do you find for sinners, including those who commit homosexual sin, in the following verses: **Isaiah 53:4–6; 1 Corinthians 15:3; 2 Corinthians 5:17–18?**

God's Claim on Our Bodies (1 Corinthians 6:12–20)

1. Paul may be quoting what some members of the church were saying, that "everything is permissible" in Christian freedom. But Paul points out that even though some things may be done, it's possible they should not be done. Read **verse 12** and **10:23** and expand upon the reasons Paul says this.

2. How does **verse 14** illustrate God's regard for the human body?

3. Think about what Paul says in **verse 15** about the Christian's body. Your body is a "member" (limb or part of the body) of Christ! Paul presents other reasons for fleeing from sexual immorality in **verses 18–20.** First, he points out that sexual sins violate our own bodies. Explain the implications of that when we remember that the Holy Spirit dwells within us.

4. As Christians we will want to honor God by the way we use our bodies. Read **Romans 6:13** and list some ways you can use your body to honor God.

The Word for Us

1. Paul speaks sarcastically when he suggests in **verse 4** that even those of "little account" in the church can judge in such "trivial matters" (that is, civil disputes among Christians). What advantages can you see in Christians settling disputes among themselves rather than resorting to civil courts?

2. In our current society, with militant gay activism practiced by some and hateful gay-bashing practiced by others, it is not easy to find the right response to homosexuals. Discuss in your group what a godly response to homosexuals would include.

3. Christ redeemed (purchased) our bodies, paying a high price **(1 Peter 1:18–19).** What implications does that have for the way we use our bodies?

Closing

Sing or speak together these stanzas of "Chief of Sinners Though I Be":

Chief of sinners though I be,
Jesus shed His blood for me,
Died that I might live on high,
Lives that I might never die.
As the branch is to the vine,
I am His, and He is mine.

O my Savior, help afford
By Your Spirit and Your Word!
When my wayward heart would stray,
Keep me in the narrow way;
Grace in time of need supply
While I live and when I die.

Lesson 7

To Marry or Not to Marry? (1 Corinthians 7:1–40)

Theme Verse

"God has called us to live in peace" **(1 Corinthians 7:15b).**

Goal

In this lesson we will grow in awareness and appreciation of marriage as God's will for most but not all believers, and we will seek to understand, accept, and observe God's will regarding divorce and remarriage.

What's Going On Here?

After his plea for unity **(chapters 1–4)** and his discussion of moral problems **(chapters 5–6),** Paul proceeds in the third portion of his letter **(chapters 7–10)** to answer questions submitted to him by the Corinthians. The questions dealt with the application of Christian freedom. In **chapter 7** the apostle dwells on matters pertaining to the question whether or not to marry. His advice represents indirect counseling, since he leaves it to the individual to decide the question on the basis of the Word of God, his or her own ability or inability to cope with sexual desires, and the unsettled conditions prevailing in the Roman Empire.

Searching the Scriptures

Read aloud or summarize **1 Corinthians 7:1–40.**

It Is Good Not to Marry If ... (1 Corinthians 7:1–9)

What the apostle writes here must be read in light of the chaotic conditions, social customs, and pagan background of the early Christian era. Paul distinguishes between the Word of God, which is permanent, and his counsel, which is contingent on circumstances. Note that this chapter does not contain all of Paul's teaching on marriage and related subjects.

1. Paul advises the Corinthian Christians not to marry. Consider the advice Paul gives to younger widows in **1 Timothy 5:14.** How does this verse help you to understand more fully Paul's overall attitude toward marriage?

2. Even though Paul says it would be sensible for the Corinthians to remain unmarried for the time, Paul recommends marriage in **1 Corinthians 7:2.** Think about what Paul says in that verse and also in **verse 5.** What awareness of human nature is Paul revealing in these verses?

3. Read **verses 3–6.** What understanding about the nature of the marriage relationship is stated in this passage?

4. In **verses 8–9** Paul repeats his counsel that the Corinthians who are unmarried remain in that situation. However, he acknowledges that some couples may be better off getting married. Describe a situation today in which you would agree, though perhaps with misgivings, that a couple should marry despite practical disadvantages.

Counsel to the Married (1 Corinthians 7:10–16)

1. Paul now speaks to those who are already married, giving what he knows is a command from the Lord **(Matthew 19:5–6),** not merely his own counsel. That command is that people are to marry for life **(vv. 10–11b).** Paul allows, however, for the possibility that a Christian might separate from her or his spouse. If a Christian does separate or divorce, Paul calls for that person to remain single or, if possible, to be reconciled to the separated spouse **(v. 11a).** In your opinion, what reasoning lies behind this direction?

2. God intended that marriage fulfill several purposes. What do the following passages say about the purposes of marriage? See **1 Corinthians 7:3–4; Genesis 1:28; 2:18.**

Accepting Life on Its Own Terms (1 Corinthians 7:17–24)

1. Paul refers to circumcision **(vv. 18–29).** Circumcision was commanded for Jews in the Old Testament as a sign of the covenant God had made with them to bring the Savior into the world through them. Explain why Paul says that someone who insists on being circumcised for spiritual reasons has fallen away from grace.

2. Paul's counsel to slaves does not mean that Paul (or the Lord) approved of slavery itself. Note what Paul says to slaves who have an opportunity to gain their freedom in **verses 21–23.** What assessment of slavery do you find revealed in this passage?

Counsel to the Unmarried (1 Corinthians 7:25–35)

1. In **verses 26, 28b,** and **32–34,** Paul states several reasons why it would be good for the virgins (unmarried women, **v. 34**) of Corinth at that time not to marry. (The "present crisis" to which Paul refers in **verse 26** may refer to the hostile environment in which the Corinthian Christians were then living.) Under what circumstances do you think these reasons would be as valid today as they were for the Corinthians in Paul's day?

2. Consider Paul's comments in **verses 29–31.** Try to put in your own words the Christian's attitude toward life in this world, which Paul expresses in this paragraph.

A Word for the Engaged and Widows (1 Corinthians 7:36–40)

1. In Paul's day a prospective husband had more control over the decision to marry than did a prospective wife. Now the decision is mutual. Notice in **verse 37** how Paul refers to a prospective bridegroom whose reasoning, rather than feelings, determines whether or not to marry. What advice might you give to enable a young person to make a thoughtful choice about marriage?

2. Think back over the chapter you have studied this week. What insight has been most important to you?

The Word for Us

1. The "concession" Paul speaks about in **1 Corinthians 7:6** refers to the freedom to choose to marry or not to marry. Although marriage is God's design as part of His creation, it is not commanded that anyone marry. To some, God gives the gift of marriage; to others He gives the gift of living a single life. What reasons might someone have for choosing to remain unmarried?

2. In what ways might a congregation meet particular needs of unmarried adults?

3. What advice does Paul give concerning a Christian's choice of a marriage partner?

4. Read what Paul has to say to the Corinthians in **verses 17** and **24** about their place in life. What do these verses contribute to your understanding about your own place in life?

5. Consider thoughtfully Paul's comments in **verses 29–31.** Try to put in your own words the Christian's attitude toward life, which Paul expresses in this paragraph.

Closing

Speak a brief prayer, perhaps a prayer of thanksgiving for the blessings God gives us through our marriages or our singleness, asking Him to enable us to serve Him wholeheartedly in that station in life to which He has called us. Then sing or speak together these stanzas of "Blest Be the Tie That Binds":

> Blest be the tie that binds
> Our hearts in Christian love;
> The unity of heart and mind
> Is like to that above.

> Before our Father's throne
> We pour our ardent prayers;
> Our fears, our hopes, our aims are one,
> Our comforts and our cares.

Lesson 8

Christian Freedom (1 Corinthians 8:1–13)

Theme Verse

"Be careful, however, that the exercise of your freedom does not become a stumbling block to the weak" **(1 Corinthians 8:9).**

Goal

In this lesson we will see how Christians are to exercise their rights in ways that do not harm others spiritually, but rather benefit them.

What's Going On Here?

Having stated principles to help the Christians in Corinth decide for themselves whether or not to marry under their circumstances **(chapter 7),** Paul continues by applying the Christian freedom theme to another question asked of him: "May Christians eat foods offered to idols?" He distinguishes three types of Christians involved in the question: (1) those who have no scruples about eating such meat because they know an idol is nothing; (2) those who regard the practice as sinful and refrain from it; and (3) those who consider the practice sinful and so violate their consciences by joining others in eating such foods anyway. Paul pleads with the strong in faith to suspend their Christian freedom, lest by their eating of foods once offered to idols they offend the weak in faith and cause spiritual harm to brethren for whom Christ died.

Searching the Scriptures

Read aloud or summarize **1 Corinthians 8:1–13.**

"Knowledge" and Love (1 Corinthians 8:1–6)

Paul moves to another subject that the Corinthians had asked about, the eating of meat offered to idols. But before he deals with specifics, he emphasizes the place of knowledge and love toward God and toward one another.

1. Paul writes in **verse 1** of himself, the Corinthians, and all Christians that "we all possess knowledge." Paul summarizes the knowledge he is referring to in **verses 4b–6.** Why is knowledge alone inadequate to a right relationship with God? (See **James 2:19.**)

2. Paul contrasts knowledge with love in **1 Corinthians 8:1b.** What do you think Paul meant by this observation?

3. Paul comes to the subject of eating food that was sacrificed to heathen idols. Compare what Paul says about these idols in **verses 4–5** with **Psalm 135:15–18.** These idols were worshiped as gods or as though they represented gods, though such "gods" actually did not exist. Idolatry is giving someone or something else the reverence and trust that belong only to the true God. Why might it be said that idolatry is still the number 1 sin?

Love to the Weak in Faith (1 Corinthians 8:7–13)

1. People in Corinth might join friends in dining rooms at one of the temples to eat meat left over from a sacrifice to a heathen god. Some of this meat also was sold in the market. Apparently, some Christians thought that the idol gods really did exist and that eating meat left over from a pagan sacrifice brought them into actual contact with these gods. Explain how Christians who thought this way would be confused by seeing other Christians eating meat sacrificed to idols.

2. Read **verses 7–13** carefully, noting the strong language Paul uses as he speaks about the careless disregard some believers in Corinth were showing weaker believers. What response do these words prompt in you?

The Word for Us

1. Read **John 1:3, 10.** Notice that the same thing stated about God the Father in **1 Corinthians 8:6a** is repeated exactly about Jesus Christ in **1 Corinthians 8:6b.** What conclusion or conclusions can you draw from that?

2. Read **Romans 14:21** and **1 Corinthians 8:13,** noting what Paul says he is willing to give up. What would you be willing to give up to avoid injuring a weak Christian's conscience (or, what have you already given up for this reason)?

3. Comment on the responsibility of the stronger Christian in regard to weaker Christians in light of the verses from **1 Corinthians 8.**

Closing

Sing or speak together these stanzas of "Jesus Shall Reign":

Jesus shall reign where'er the sun
Does its successive journeys run;
His kingdom stretch from shore to shore
Till moons shall wax and wane no more.

To Him shall endless prayer be made,
And praises throng to crown His head;
His name like sweet perfume shall rise
With ev'ry morning sacrifice.

Lesson 9

Your Rights and the Needs of Others (1 Corinthians 9:1–27)

Theme Verses

"I make myself a slave to everyone. ... I do all this for the sake of the gospel, that I may share in its blessings" **(1 Corinthians 9:19, 23).**

Goal

In this lesson we will see how in some cases using our Christian rights and freedom to the full extent may help us to share Christ more effectively. In other cases, foregoing the exercise of those rights may be more helpful. In love and consideration for those we are trying to reach, and in faithfulness to God, we will decide on the basis of what promises to be most beneficial.

What's Going On Here?

Enemies in Corinth may have said, "Paul is preaching the Gospel because it gives him an income." To dispose of this suggestion, the apostle personalizes the previously discussed principles of Christian freedom and Christian love. He demonstrates how in his own life he set aside his rights (to eat and drink, to marry, to draw a salary) that he might carry out his grand design to gain all people for the Gospel. His closing remarks encourage the Corinthians to follow his example in practicing self-discipline, lest preoccupation with individual rights and conveniences interfere with faith and its glorious goal.

Searching the Scriptures

Read aloud or summarize **1 Corinthians 9:1–27.**

Rights of a Duly Called Apostle
(1 Corinthians 9:1–12a, 13–14)

1. Paul now gives an example of knowing one's rights but voluntarily laying them down. Read **Acts 22:4–16.** How did this experience qualify Paul to be an apostle?

2. Paul also points to the Corinthian congregation as a "seal" of his apostleship. What do you think he means by that? (A seal is an official imprinted mark that certifies a document as genuine.)

3. What impresses you about how Paul refers to his office on the one hand and, on the other hand, to himself as a person?

4. Paul refers to two rights he might claim as an apostle in **1 Corinthians 9:4–6.** What are they?

Rights Sacrificed for the Gospel
(1 Corinthians 9:12b, 15–18)

1. Read **1 Corinthians 9:12–19.** Despite the fact that Paul maintains as a scriptural principle that those who labor in the ministry of the church are to receive their livelihood from their work, Paul himself did not usually accept this support. Why do you think Paul did not use his right of support?

2. Why do you think Paul felt compelled to preach the Gospel? Read **1 Corinthians 9:16–17** and **Acts 26:15–18** and explain Paul's thinking.

3. Under what circumstances today might a minister of the Gospel (pastor, teacher, or other professional church worker) earn his or her livelihood in another way, so as to carry on the Gospel ministry without cost (or at minimal cost) to the church?

Rights Sacrificed to Attain the Goal
(1 Corinthians 9:19–27)

1. What do you think Paul is referring to when he insists that he is "free" (**vv. 1, 19**)?

2. Paul is free, but he makes himself a slave. What do you think Paul means when he says that he makes himself a slave to everyone?

The Word for Us

1. What application do you think **1 Corinthians 9:4–6** has to church workers today?

2. Paul willingly makes himself a slave in order to share in the blessings of the Gospel **(v. 23)**. What blessings are you receiving from the Gospel?

3. Paul's goal was to win as many as possible. To accomplish this he was willing to do anything he could. What specific things do you think you might do to win people for Christ?

Closing

Sing or speak together these stanzas of " 'Come, Follow Me,' Said Christ, the Lord":

"Come, follow Me," said Christ, the Lord,
"All in My way abiding;
Your selfishness throw overboard,
Obey My call and guiding.
Oh, bear your crosses, and confide
In My example as your guide."

Then let us follow Christ, our Lord,
And take the cross appointed
And, firmly clinging to His word,
In suff'ring be undaunted.
For those who bear the battle's strain
The crown of heav'nly life obtain.

Lesson 10

Taking Temptation Seriously (1 Corinthians 10:1–33)

Theme Verse

"God is faithful; He will not let you be tempted beyond what you can bear. But when you are tempted, He will also provide a way out so that you can stand up under it" (**1 Corinthians 10:13**).

Goal

In this lesson we will become more aware of the seriousness of temptations. God promises that we will not be tempted beyond our ability to endure. God always provides a way out of temptation through Jesus Christ.

What's Going On Here?

In **chapter 10,** Paul warns against participation in idol worship. Paul previously allowed that discerning Christians have the freedom, barring the giving of offense to the weak in faith, to eat food offered to idols. But it is one thing to eat such food in private homes and quite another thing to participate in idol worship. Paul adds the lesson that idolatry itself is a sin and must be shunned. It is wrong to argue that an idol is nothing. For in idolatry the devil is worshiped.

Searching the Scriptures

Read aloud or summarize **1 Corinthians 10:1–33.**

People of Israel Not Immune to Idolatry (1 Corinthians 10:1–13)

1. Paul devotes a section of his letter to warn about temptation. He uses examples from history, specifically the journey of Israel in Egypt to freedom in the Promised Land. Read a little about the Old Testament events, to which Paul refers. As you do, make note of anything that's new or surprising to you.

2. Israel's example stands as a warning for us. What four sins in particular drew down God's wrath on them?

Verse 7 (Exodus 32:1–6)

Verse 8 (Numbers 25:1–3)

Verse 9 (Exodus 17:1–2)

Verse 10 (Numbers 16:1–3)

Corinthians Shun Idolatry (1 Corinthians 10:14–22)

1. Why does Paul bring up the topic of Holy Communion in his discussion of idolatry? In other words, how do the truths about Holy Communion back up his urgent command that God's people flee idolatry?

2. When the Corinthians received the Lord's Supper, they each took a bit of bread from one loaf (v. 17). Explain the implication that Paul draws from the fact that the believers all shared "one loaf."

3. Those who sacrifice to idols really are worshiping demons (v. 20). What new implication does Paul make here?

Seeking the Good of Others (1 Corinthians 10:23–33)

1. Paul returns to the issue of eating meat offered to idols and repeats in almost the same language (v. 23) what he had said in 1 Corinthians 6:12. Everything is "permissible"—but not everything is beneficial or constructive. How are these criteria related to the principle of Christian love?

2. Read 1 Corinthians 10:24 and Galatians 6:2–5. Then express in your own words what Paul calls "the law of Christ."

3. Follow Paul's line of thought in **1 Corinthians 10:25–30.** Why does Paul say it is all right to eat meat bought in the marketplace, whether it was offered to idols or not?

The Word for Us

1. Paul warns us that we can be tempted to sin against God in the same way the Israelites did. Even the strongest Christian can be overcome by temptation. But Paul also records a promise God makes to His children when they are tempted. Read **1 Corinthians 10:12–13.** What is God saying to you personally in this passage?

2. Are you tempted to commit the sin of idolatry? Explain. (Remember that idolatry involves giving anything or anyone the trust and allegiance that rightly belongs to God alone.)

3. When you are tempted to toy with idolatry, how could you intentionally "flee" from it?

4. Note Paul's reference in **1 Corinthians 10:22** to arousing the Lord's jealousy. The Lord is jealous in that He will not share us with any other gods. We belong to Him; we have been redeemed by the blood of His Son. Participating in the Lord's Supper while holding back a part of ourselves for other "gods" arouses His jealousy. How might we prepare ourselves to receive the Lord's Supper with complete devotion?

5. Paul commands that everything, even everyday actions like eating and drinking, be done to God's glory **(1 Corinthians 10:31).** How might God be glorified in our eating and drinking?

Closing

Speak or sing together these stanzas from "What Is the World to Me":

What is the world to me
With all its vaunted pleasure
When You, and You alone,
Lord Jesus, are my treasure!
You only, dearest Lord,
My soul's delight shall be;
You are my peace, my rest.
What is the world to me!

What is the world to me!
My Jesus is my treasure,
My life, my health, my wealth,
My friend, my love, my pleasure,
My joy, my crown, my all,
My bliss eternally.
Once more, then, I declare:
What is the world to me!

Lesson 11

The Lord's Supper with Reverence (1 Corinthians 11:1–34)

Theme Verse

"Whoever eats the bread or drinks the cup of the Lord in an unworthy manner will be guilty of sinning against the body and blood of the Lord" (**1 Corinthians 11:27**).

Goal

In this chapter, Paul looks at the temptation to be disrespectful to those whom God has placed in authority over us. He ends his list of examples with the temptation to violate the Lord's Supper. We need to be alert to these temptations, to guard against them, and to take the full advantage of the way out of temptation, which God always provides in Jesus Christ.

What's Going On Here?

From here to the end of **chapter 14,** Paul deals with good order that should prevail in public worship. Paul rebukes the Corinthians for improper conduct shown at their services. The particular abuses referred to are improper dress and unbecoming behavior of women, as well as abuses in the administration of the Lord's Supper.

Searching the Scriptures

Read aloud or summarize **1 Corinthians 11:1–34.**

Women and Men at Worship (1 Corinthians 11:2–16)

1. Paul urges the Corinthians to follow his example, as he himself follows the example of Christ **(11:1).** What did Paul have in mind in saying that he followed the example of Christ? (Compare **10:33** and **Matthew 20:28.**)

2. Customs and practices often express principles or fundamental truths. In such cases, it is the principle or fundamental truth that is enduring, and not necessarily the custom or practice. That is the situation in the matter of head coverings, which Paul discusses in this section. Customs may change, while the fundamental truths they reflect do not. Carefully consider **verses 2–10.** What do you think is Paul's main concern in this passage?

3. The roles of men and women in relationship to one another are rooted in creation (and so apply to all, whether believers or not). Christians will desire to conform to God's created order because they honor God and because they do not wish to bring the Christian faith into disrepute. However, Paul also refers in **verses 11–12** to another principle rooted in salvation. He expresses this salvation principle more clearly in **Galatians 3:26–29.** State this principle in your own words.

The Love Feast (1 Corinthians 11:17–26)

1. Paul praised the Corinthians in **verse 2,** but in **verse 17** he has "no praise" for them. Consider **verses 17–22** and state in your own words Paul's objections to their behavior.

2. How was the way the church at Corinth observed the Lord's Supper having just the opposite effect you would expect it to have on the believers' relationships with one another?

Admonition to Communicants (1 Corinthians 11:27–34)

1. Paul has strong things to say about eating and drinking the Lord's Supper in an "unworthy manner" **(v. 27),** "without recognizing the body of the Lord" **(v. 29).** Notice that taking part unworthily is a sin against the Lord's body and blood. Paul recommends that we examine ourselves before taking part in the Lord's Supper. What might we ask our Lord to reveal to us in such an examination?

2. What preparation have you found especially helpful toward receiving the Lord's Supper with blessing?

The Word for Us

1. **1 Corinthians 11:2–16** does not define the roles of men and women in every possible life situation. Rather, Paul talks about how we express these roles in the public worship service. Why is it important for Christian women (and men, as well) to conform to accepted customs that define morality and modesty?

2. While the Bible does not say how often we are to take part in the Lord's Supper, **verse 26** implies that this is to happen frequently. What benefits do you see in a frequent partaking of the Lord's Supper?

Closing

Speak or sing together these stanzas from "Jesus, Your Blood and Righteousness":

Jesus, Your blood and righteousness
My beauty are, my glorious dress;
Mid flaming worlds, in these arrayed,
With joy shall I lift up my head.

Bold shall I stand in that great day,
Cleansed and redeemed, no debt to pay;
For by Your cross absolved I am
From sin and guilt, from fear and shame.

Lesson 12

Spiritual Gifts
(1 Corinthians 12–13)

Theme Verse

"To each one the manifestation of the Spirit is given for the common good" **(1 Corinthians 12:7).**

Goal

In this lesson we will see how all Christians are blessed by the Holy Spirit with special abilities called "spiritual gifts" and view these gifts as equipment for spiritual service to God and one another.

What's Going On Here?

Having discussed good order at public worship and the proper observance of the Lord's Supper **(chapter 11),** Paul proceeds to another point of church order, namely, the nature and use of spiritual gifts. The Holy Spirit, who leads people to faith in Jesus Christ, also gives them a variety of gifts. With these gifts, Christians are enabled to render a variety of services for the common good of the church. While by God's order some offices in the church rank higher than others and carry more responsibilities, every member who serves the body of Christ, in whatever capacity, is to be held in honor.

Searching the Scriptures

Read aloud or summarize **1 Corinthians 12–13.**

Faith and Other Gifts of the Spirit
(1 Corinthians 12:1–11)

1. Paul now takes up another subject that he apparently had been asked about—spiritual gifts. A simple definition of a spiritual gift is "an ability given by the Spirit that enables a Christian to serve the Lord and the needs of others in the church." Summarize Paul's main point in **verses 4–6.**

2. Who receives spiritual gifts?

3. The spiritual gift of wisdom enables a Christian to be especially effective in communicating God's wisdom to others. Read **1 Corinthians 1:23–24; 2:6–8.** What is this wisdom all about?

The Human Body: Example of a Coordinated Whole
(1 Corinthians 12:12–20)

1. Read **1 Corinthians 12:14–20** again. Put into your own words the point Paul makes in this paragraph. Then apply that point to yourself as a member of Christ's body.

2. The human body feels and acts as a unit. By what actions does the body of Christ demonstrate that it, too, is a unit?

3. Some spiritual gifts have greater importance in God's kingdom (**v. 30;** see also **14:1, 5, 12**). What does Jesus tell us about greatness among His followers?

The Qualities of Christian Love
(1 Corinthians 13:1–13)

1. **Chapter 13 (vv. 1–3)** begins by comparing love to several of the spiritual gifts mentioned in **chapter 12.** What makes love superior to those gifts?

2. **Verses 4–7** in **chapter 13** define love by how it acts. Compare the love Paul describes with the way love is generally presented in our own culture today.

3. Our knowledge of God and our ability to tell others everything about Him will remain incomplete or imperfect until perfection comes (**vv. 9–10**). The word *perfect* here means complete, fulfilled. How are knowing and being known by God in a personal relationship with Him related to one another (**v. 12b**)?

The Word for Us

1. Before they became Christians, the Corinthians thought pagan idols were their lords **(12:2).** But now they called Jesus "Lord." What does **1 Corinthians 12:3** say about the role of the Holy Spirit regarding your own faith in Jesus?

2. Under what circumstances might the exercise of even God-given gifts cause trouble in a Christian congregation today?

3. Notice in **1 Corinthians 13:12** what Paul is anticipating when perfection is a reality. What are you looking forward to seeing or knowing when everything has been made perfect in the world to come?

4. Faith, hope, and love remain, Paul says. These three often are spoken about together or in different combinations. Why is love the greatest of the three?

Closing

Sing or speak together these stanzas of "Holy Spirit, Light Divine":

Holy Spirit, light divine,
Dawn upon this soul of mine;
Let Your word dispel the night,
Wake my spirit, clear my sight.

Holy Spirit, all divine,
Dwell within this self of mine;
I Your temple pure would be
Now and for eternity.

Lesson 13

Meaningful Worship
(1 Corinthians 14:1–40)

Theme Verse

"When you come together, everyone has a hymn, or a word of instruction, a revelation, a tongue or an interpretation. All of these must be done for the strengthening of the church" **(1 Corinthians 14:26)**.

Goal

Because God wants to bless His people in Christ as they gather to worship Him, God's people have a wonderful potential for meaningful worship.

What's Going On Here?

Paul would prefer that worship leaders and participants prophesy, that is, speak the Word of God in language that all can understand. But because he recognizes speaking in tongues as a gift of the Holy Spirit, Paul does not forbid its use in the church. However, he does feel it necessary to point out the limitations of such speaking and to outline the condition necessary for orderly worship. Peace and good order will prevail in public worship when Christians make the love of God's Word and for one another their aim.

Searching the Scriptures

Read aloud or summarize **1 Corinthians 14:1–40**.

Mere Sounds Do Not Edify the Church
(1 Corinthians 14:1–13)

1. Paul refers to prophecy as a gift to "desire" **(v. 1)**. What reason does

he cite for this **(vv. 1–4)?**

2. Paul contrasts prophecy and speaking in tongues and points out some limitations of speaking in tongues. Note especially **verses 2, 4,** and **11.** What do these verses tell you about Paul's priority for what happens when Christians gather for worship?

3. What are Paul's two main concerns regarding the gift of tongues? (You may want to refer to **chapter 12.**)

Praying with Spirit and Mind
(1 Corinthians 14:14–21)

1. A person who was speaking in a tongue without being able to understand it himself was not using his mind **(vv. 14–17).** What do Paul's comments in these verses tell you about the use of the mind in our spiritual life?

2. Paul tells the Christians of Corinth to stop thinking like children, except when it comes to evil. What do you think he means by saying that Christians are to be infants in regard to evil **(v. 20)?**

3. What is meant by the phrase "in your thinking be adults," especially as we value and use our spiritual gifts?

Let Order Prevail (1 Corinthians 14:22–33)

1. In **verses 22–23,** Paul refers to the impact of unintelligible tongues on unbelievers who would visit the services held by the Corinthians. How would hearing unintelligible tongues affect these unbelievers **(v. 23)?**

2. Consider the rule Paul lays down about the inclusion of speaking in tongues in **verses 27–28.** How does this rule fit in with what he wrote in **verse 26b?**

3. Note the three specific instructions Paul gives for the use of prophecy in the worship service **(vv. 29–33a).** Is orderliness still a concern in the conduct of public worship services?

Paul's Instruction by Divine Authority (1 Corinthians 14:34–40)

1. Paul speaks to the issue of proper decorum in the worship service as it applies to the roles of men and women. He previously addressed this issue in **11:3–16.** Review your study of that earlier passage, and note Paul's comment in **verse 34** regarding the requirement of the Law. Notice also Paul's concluding comment in **verse 40.** What is fitting about a respectful reserve on the part of women in public worship?

2. As women are called on to respectfully yield to men in the home and in the church, men are called on to respectfully honor women **(1 Peter 3:7; 1 Corinthians 11:11–12; Ephesians 5:25– 33).** What does such

respectful treatment of women by Christian men communicate to unbelievers?

The Word for Us

1. In order to correct the confusion in Corinth about the use of tongues in worship, Paul urges the person who has the gift to pray also for the gift of interpreting or translating the language **(v. 13)**. What does this suggest to an individual Christian or to a congregation that thinks it lacks certain gifts that it needs?

2. Paul declares that in worship he would rather speak five intelligible words that instruct, rather than 10,000 words in an unintelligible tongue **(v. 19)**. What implications might Paul's statement have for a preacher or teacher in the church today?

3. In **verse 26,** Paul lists various elements of worship and speaks about their purpose in the service. What in this verse would be especially helpful to those who plan worship services?

4. Paul, in **verse 28,** does not permit speaking in tongues in public services without interpretation. What does this tell you about the place of the gift of tongues in public worship?

5. Christians are not to go off on their own tangents, ignoring the effect their behavior has on others **(v. 36)**. Paul maintains that what he has written about conducting worship in an orderly and fitting way is not his own personal opinion but was written by the Lord's command. What does this say to the idea that what Paul has written no longer applies to us today?

Closing

Sing or speak together these stanzas of "Alleluia! Let Praises Ring":

Alleluia! Let praises ring!
To God the Father let us bring
Our songs of adoration.
To Him through everlasting days
Be worship, honor, pow'r, and praise,
Whose hand sustains creation.
Singing, Ringing:
Holy, holy, God is holy;
Spread the story
Of our God, the Lord of glory.

Alleluia! Let praises ring!
Unto our triune God we sing;
Blest be His name forever!
With angel hosts let us adore
And sing His praises more and more
For all His grace and favor!
Singing, Ringing:
Holy, holy, God is holy;
Spread the story
Of our God, the Lord of glory!

Lesson 14

Hope in the Resurrection (1 Corinthians 15–16)

Theme Verse

"So will it be with the resurrection of the dead. The body that is sown is perishable, it is raised imperishable" (**1 Corinthians 15:42**).

Goal

In this lesson we will see that through faith in the promise of the resurrection, we can face both death and life with great confidence.

What's Going On Here?

From problems of disunity (**chapters 1–4**), immorality (**chapters 5–6**), the use of Christian freedom (**chapters 7–10**), and public worship (**chapters 11–14**), Paul turns his attention in **chapter 15** to a new subject on which the Corinthians need instruction—the doctrine of the resurrection. He lays the foundation for his discussion by first establishing the resurrection of Jesus Christ as attested by the Old Testament and living witnesses of New Testament times. In two sections (**1 Corinthians 15:12–19, 29–34**), he dwells on absurdities that follow from denial of the resurrection of the dead. He bases belief in the resurrection on Christ's conquest of death as proclaimed by His resurrection and exaltation. He anticipates and answers the questions of how the dead are raised and with what kind of bodies. After a revelation-supported, declaration of faith in the Christian's victory over death, he urges the Corinthians to maintain a steadfast, fruitful, and hopeful faith.

In **chapter 16**, Paul discusses the Corinthians' inquiry about the collection for the poor in Jerusalem. Other matters of importance for Christian fellowship follow. In the closing portion of his letter, Paul includes an announcement of his plans for the immediate future, references to Timothy and Apollos as co-workers, encouragement to steadfast faith and fervent love, a request in behalf of the household of Stephanas, and brotherly greetings.

Searching the Scriptures

Read aloud or summarize **1 Corinthians 15:1–16:24.**

Witness Bearers of the Resurrection (1 Corinthians 15:1–11)

1. Paul reminds the Corinthians of the Gospel he had preached to them. Review **verses 3–5.** What are the main points of the Gospel as stated in these verses?

2. In addition to prophecies in the Old Testament, Paul points to the testimony of eyewitnesses in declaring that Jesus rose from death. Why do you think the testimony of eyewitnesses would be important in establishing that Jesus had risen from death?

3. Paul says that everything he is has come about as the result of God's grace, God's unmerited favor. Read **verses 9–11.** How do these verses help to explain what Paul means by "grace"?

Christ Has Conquered Death (1 Corinthians 15:12–34)

1. Some of the Corinthian Christians questioned the resurrection of the dead. Read what Paul says about this in **verses 14–19** and summarize his argument for the resurrection.

2. Paul writes that Christ must reign until He has put all His enemies under His feet. He writes that the last such enemy is death. When Christ comes again in His power and glory and raises all the dead, there will be no more dying; death will be a thing of the past. How is Christ now reigning until that event takes place? (See **Colossians 1:18; 3:15a; Hebrews 8:1–2.**)

3. In **verse 29,** Paul mentions being baptized for the dead. This passage is puzzling and, while we may guess at its meaning, we cannot be certain. Read **Mark 16:16** and **Hebrews 9:27.** Why would those passages rule out an interpretation of **1 Corinthians 15:29** that teaches that Christians may be baptized on behalf of someone who has already died?

Rising with Glorified Bodies
(1 Corinthians 15:35–58)

1. Paul now takes up the subject of what our bodies will be like after the resurrection. What three comparisons does Paul use to illustrate our resurrected bodies?

2. Since the natural, perishable body cannot inherit the kingdom of God, Christ will change our mortal bodies when He returns in glory at the end of time. What do **verses 50–52** say about this change?

3. Paul concludes **chapter 15** by encouraging his brothers to stand firm and to give themselves fully to the Lord's work. What is the connection between the resurrection of Christ and Paul's words of encouragement in **verse 58?**

Christian Giving (1 Corinthians 16:1–24)

1. Paul turns to a practical matter, the completion of a collection for the poor believers in Jerusalem. What are the reasons for their suffering (see **Acts 9:1–2; 11:28**)?

2. In **verses 13–14,** Paul speaks some final strong words of admonition and encouragement. What are the five things he encourages?

3. Think of those who devote themselves to the "service of the saints" **(v. 15)** in your congregation (pastors, staff support, and laypeople). What do you think Paul has in mind when he urges the congregation to "submit" **(v. 16)** to these people?

The Word for Us

1. Paul says that the Corinthians believed and took their stand on this Gospel. How does your life show that you also have, by God's grace, believed and taken your stand on this Gospel?

2. If Christ had not been raised, what effect would that have on your faith?

3. What can you learn from **1 Corinthians 15:36–38** regarding our bodies after the resurrection?

4. While the collection to which Paul refers was a one-time offering, we can learn from it principles we can apply to our own week-by-week giving for the Lord's work. List them from **1 Corinthians 16:2.**

Closing

Speak or sing together these stanzas from "Jesus Lives! The Victory's Won":

Jesus lives! The vict'ry's won!
Death no longer can appall me;
Jesus lives! Death's reign is done!
From the grave will Christ recall me.
Brighter scenes will then commence;
This shall be my confidence.

Jesus lives! And I am sure
Neither life nor death shall sever
Me from Him. I shall endure
In His love, through death, forever.
God will be my sure defense;
This shall be my confidence.

1 CORINTHIANS
One in Christ

Leaders Notes

Preparing to Teach 1 Corinthians

In preparation to teach, consult the introduction to the book of 1 Corinthians in the *Concordia Self-Study Bible*, and if possible, read the *Concordia Self-Study Commentary* (CPH, 1979).

Also read the text in a modern translation. The NIV is generally referred to in the lesson comments.

In the section "Searching the Scriptures," the leader guides discussion, using the questions given (or others) to help the class discover what the text actually says. This is a major part of teaching, namely, directing the learners to discover for themselves.

Another major portion of each lesson is "The Word for Us." This section helps participants, through discussion, to see the meaning of the text for our times, for church and world today, and especially for our own lives.

Group Bible Study

Group Bible study means mutual learning from one another under the guidance of a leader or facilitator. The Bible is an inexhaustible resource. No one person can discover all it has to offer. In a class many eyes see many things and can apply them to many life situations. The leader should resist the temptation to "give the answers" and so act as an "authority." This teaching approach stifles participation by individual members and can actually hamper learning. As a general rule the teacher is not to "give interpretation" but to "develop interpreters." Of course there are times when the leader should and must share insights and information gained by his or her own deeper research. The ideal class is one in which the leader guides class members through the lesson and engages them in meaningful sharing and discussion at all points, leading them to a summary of the lesson at the close. As a general rule, don't explain what the learners can discover by themselves.

Have a chalkboard and chalk or newsprint and marker available to emphasize significant points of the lesson. Put your inquiries or the inquiries of participants into questions, problems, or issues. This provokes thought. Keep discussion to the point. List on the chalkboard or newsprint the answers given. Then determine the most vital points made in the discussion. Ask additional questions to fill apparent gaps.

The aim of every Bible study is to help people grow spiritually, not merely in biblical and theological knowledge, but in Christian thinking and living. This means growth in Christian attitudes, insights, and skills for Christian living. The focus of this course must be the church and the world of our day. The guiding question will be, "What does the Lord teach us for life today through the book of 1 Corinthians?"

Pace Your Teaching

Do not try to cover every question in each lesson. This will lead to undue haste and frustration. Be selective. Pace your teaching. Spend no more than 5 to 10 minutes with "Theme Verse," "Goal," and "What's Going On Here?" Take time to go into the text by topic, but not word by word. Occasionally stop to help the class gain understanding of a word or concept. Allow approximately 10 to 15 minutes for "The Word for Us." Spending approximately five minutes for "Closing" and announcements, you will notice, allows you only approximately 30 minutes for "Searching the Scriptures."

Should your group have more than a one-hour class period, you can take it more leisurely. But do not allow any lesson to "drag" and become tiresome. Keep it moving. Keep it alive. Keep it meaningful. Eliminate some questions and restrict yourself to those questions most meaningful to the members of the class. If most members study the text at home, they can report their findings, and the time gained can be applied to relating the lesson to life.

Good Preparation

Good preparation by the leader usually affects the pleasure and satisfaction the class will experience.

Suggestions to the Leader for Using the Study Guide

The Lesson Pattern

This set of 14 lessons is based on a significant and timely New Testament book—1 Corinthians. The material is designed to aid Bible study, that is, to aid a consideration of the written Word of God, with discussion and personal application growing out of the text at hand.

The typical lesson is divided into six sections:
1. Theme Verse
2. Goal
3. What's Going On Here?
4. Searching the Scriptures
5. The Word for Us
6. Closing

"Theme Verse," "Goal," and "What's Going On Here?" give the leader assistance in arousing the interest of the group in the concepts of the chapter. Current events and conditions are cited to "warm up" the class and convince its members that the Word of God spoken through 1 Corinthians is relevant to their present situation. Here the leader stimulates minds. Do not linger too long over the introductory remarks. You merely show that the verses to be studied are meaningful to Christian faith and life today.

"Searching the Scriptures" provides the real "spade work" necessary for Bible study. Here the class digs, uncovers, and discovers; it gets the facts and observes them. Comment from the leader is needed only to the extent that it helps the group understand the text. The same is true of looking up the indicated parallel passages. The questions in the Study Guide, arranged under subheadings and corresponding to sections within the text, are intended to help the participants discover the meaning of the text.

Having determined what the text says, the class is ready to apply the message. Having heard, read, marked, and learned the Word of God, proceed to digest it inwardly through discussion, evaluation, and application. This is done, as the Study Guide suggests, by taking the truths found in 1 Corinthians and applying them to the world and Christianity, in general, and then to personal Christian life. Class time may not permit discussion of all questions and topics. In preparation the leader may need to select two or three and focus on them. These questions bring God's message to the individual Christian. Close the session by reviewing one important truth from the lesson.

Remember, the Word of God is sacred, but the Study Guide is not. The guide offers only suggestions. The leader should not hesitate to alter the guidelines or substitute others to meet his or her needs and the needs of the participants. Adapt your teaching plan to your class and your class period. Good teaching directs the learner to discover for himself or herself. For the teacher this means directing the learner, not giving the learner answers. As you prepare, mark those sections that suggest a class activity. Choose the verses that should be looked up in Scripture. What discussion questions will you ask? at what points? Write them in the margin of your study book. Involve class members but give them clear directions.

How will you best use your teaching period? Do you have 45 minutes? an hour? or 1½ hours? If time is short, what should you cut? Learn to become a wise steward of class time.

Be sure to take time to summarize the lesson or have a class member do it. Remember to pray frequently for yourself and your class.

Lesson 1

The Power of Forgiveness
(1 Corinthians 1:1–31)

Theme Verse

Invite a volunteer to read the theme verse for this lesson.

Goal

Read aloud the goal statement. Point out that the goal will briefly describe the direction the lesson will take.

What's Going On Here?

Read aloud or have a volunteer read aloud this introductory section.

Searching the Scriptures

Read aloud or have volunteers read aloud **1 Corinthians 1.** You may wish to have participants discuss the questions in small groups, if your class is large. If you divide your class into small groups, allow time for the groups to share the answers to the questions with the entire class.

Paul's Greeting (1 Corinthians 1:1–3)

1. Paul wrote with the authority of an apostle. The authority of his God-given office would be especially important when it came to asserting the strong rebukes and warnings Paul needed to deliver to the Corinthians. They would know that he was expressing not just his personal opinion but a judgment spoken with the authority of Christ Jesus Himself and by the will of God.

2. God Himself has made us holy by the saving work of Jesus. God's grace removes our sins for the sake of the payment Jesus made on the cross, and God gives us the holiness of Jesus. We receive this holiness and sanctifying through faith, which also is the work of God the Holy Spirit. In this faith we cling to God's Gospel Word, the truth that is centered in Jesus, our Savior.

3. Paul had heard about some of the problems in Corinth from members of the "Chloe's household" **(1:11)** and had received a request from the church asking for his counsel **(7:1a).** He also was able to talk to three members of the congregation—Stephanas, Fortunatus, and Achaicus—who evidently delivered the letter **(16:17).**

Paul's Thanksgiving (1 Corinthians 1:4–17)

1. Paul mentions specifically that God had given the Corinthians His grace; that they were "enriched in every way," in speaking and knowledge—the congregation evidently enjoyed rich teaching, practical and devotional understanding, pastoral guidance, and theological depth; that Paul's testimony about Jesus had been confirmed and made strong in them as a result of his preaching; and that the congregation did not lack any spiritual gift.

2. When Jesus returns, the church will be blameless, because God who is faithful keeps it in the cleansing flow of His grace.

3. The four factions in the Corinthian congregation claimed to follow Paul, Apollos, Cephas, and Christ. There is no notion as to how large each group was nor whether everyone in the congregation was a member of one of these factions. The factions usually result from personality cliques.

The Cross, God's Way of Salvation (1 Corinthians 1:18–25)

1. We need saving because we are by nature without the righteousness God requires, and we cannot achieve it by our own efforts. Without that righteousness, however, we are lost in eternal spiritual death.

2. God saved us through the perfect life Jesus lived for us and the substitutionary death He died for us on the cross. By Christ's sacrifice, we are reconciled to God and are at peace with Him.

3. Jesus' death on the cross was necessary to pay for our sin. In exchange for our sins, Jesus gives us His own righteousness.

God's Action in Corinth (1 Corinthians 1:26–31)

1. God's cause makes progress because of God's power, not because of human efforts. This becomes evident when we see that the Gospel advanced without any of the usual human explanations for that advance.

2. God did not want believers to have an excuse to boast **(1:28–29).** Rather, He wanted them to be convinced that their faith rests only on His power, not on any merit or worth in themselves or in other people **(2:5).**

3. The Gospel is for everyone and is relevant to the needs of everyone, no matter where they are in life. We all need the Gospel. People from every economic and social class do hear and receive the Gospel with faith. This was true in Paul's day, and it's true in ours. Nevertheless, the Gospel sometimes seems to make more progress among some groups of people than others.

The Word for Us

1. Despite the serious problems that caused Paul much distress, anguish, and tears, he wrote in love and wanted the Corinthians to know

the "depth of my love for you" **(2 Corinthians 2:4)**. Such attitudes always go a long way toward resolving serious and sensitive problems such as those that confronted the congregation at Corinth. Churches today also are plagued by problems. Genuine concern, patience, and love will go a long way in resolving them.

2. Encourage the group to be specific in thanking God for things about their congregation—not just for the pastor and leaders, but for specific strengths God has built into your congregation and opportunities He has given you for mission.

3. Factions usually result from personality cliques. They often cause divisions and quarrels in the congregation. Such activities get in the way of the church's task of making disciples of Jesus by baptizing and teaching and will often discourage and offend new or weak Christians. They may even cause someone to lose his or her personal faith.

4a. While Baptism is part of bringing people to faith, it also begins the process of nurture, the task of encouraging and assisting growth in faith and Christian living. Paul held Baptism in high regard, but he regarded this task as given primarily to others who would build on his evangelistic work.

b. Underscore the fact that all God's people can be actively engaged in both evangelism and nurture as they pray and also as they give of themselves in both formal programs and informal words and action in their daily living.

5. The message is God's message, and the power that works through the message is God's power. This realization is a wonderful assurance for the person who is attempting to communicate the Gospel to others. We are responsible for communicating the message as clearly as we can; the effect of the message we deliver and whether it is received or rejected is not our responsibility.

Closing

Sing or speak together the closing hymn printed in the Study Guide. Ask participants for prayer concerns or requests. Pray or have a volunteer pray for those things identified by the participants.

Lesson 2

Wisdom from the Holy Spirit
(1 Corinthians 2:1–16)

Theme Verses

Invite a volunteer to read the theme verses for this lesson.

Goal

Read aloud the goal statement. Point out that the goal will briefly describe the direction the lesson will take.

What's Going On Here?

Read aloud or have a volunteer read aloud this introductory section.

Searching the Scriptures

Read aloud or have volunteers read aloud the portions of Scripture before discussing the questions.

Paul's Message of the Cross (1 Corinthians 2:1–5)

1. Paul's preaching, he himself says, was characterized by weakness, fear, and trembling, not persuasive words **(2:3–4)**.

2. Paul preached Christ crucified, and that message carried God's power. Here he refers to that power as the "Spirit's power" **(2:4)**.

God the Author of the Gospel (1 Corinthians 2:6–16)

1. God planned the salvation of the world from eternity **(v. 7)**. The failure of human reason to understand God's plan on its own is seen in the crucifixion of Jesus, God's Son. Anyone who truly had understood God's plan would not have crucified Jesus but would have welcomed Him and obediently followed Him as did the disciples, who had acted under the influence of the Spirit, not human wisdom.

2. People can't come to faith or remain in the faith on their own because (a) without the Spirit's work, a person cannot understand the Gospel and regards it as foolishness **(1 Corinthians 2:14)**; (b) by nature people are dead (unresponsive) to God and, instead, respond only to the cravings and ideas that are opposed to God and that provoke God to anger **(Ephesians 2:1–5)**; (c) the mind controlled by the sinful nature is set against God, rebels against God's will revealed in the Law, and seeks death (separation from God) rather than life with God **(Romans 8:6–8)**.

The Word for Us

1. We will want to prepare ourselves for our task by learning to present our thoughts in a clear and meaningful way. But Christians know that the Gospel we communicate is carried along by the power of the Holy Spirit and has its own persuasive power. Our witnessing must focus on Christ crucified. This is its real power.

2. Christian maturity is seen in the very opposite of the behavior that Paul describes. Mature Christians desire to dig deeply into the Word of God and to grow in their understanding of that Word. Christian maturity also will show itself in love, a forgiving spirit, patience, kindness to others, and similar Christian attitudes.

3. In regard to our salvation, God's wisdom and power are focused in Christ. Invite the group to share personal insights.

Closing

Close by singing or speaking together the hymn stanzas printed in the Study Guide. Ask participants for prayer concerns or requests. Pray or have a volunteer pray for those things identified by the participants.

Lesson 3

Jesus Christ, the Sure Foundation
(1 Corinthians 3:1–23)

Theme Verse

Invite a volunteer to read the theme verse for this lesson.

Goal

Read aloud the goal statement. Point out that the goal will briefly describe the direction the lesson will take.

What's Going On Here?

Read aloud or have a volunteer read aloud this introductory section.

Searching the Scriptures

Read aloud or have volunteers read aloud the portions of Scripture before discussing the questions.

Christian Immaturity (1 Corinthians 3:1–4)

1. Paul refers to Christians at various stages of growth or development. Giving immature Christians milk means to instruct them in the basic teachings of the Gospel until they have incorporated these teachings into their attitudes and way of life. Then these Christians may begin to take in more difficult teachings and assume a greater responsibility for the work of God's kingdom, including the teaching and guidance of those less mature in the faith.

2. In **Acts 20:32,** it is the "word of His grace" that is able to build up the immature Christian. According to **Ephesians 4:11–16,** God gives the church special "people-gifts": apostles, prophets, evangelists, pastors, and teachers. Their task is to build up the body of Christ and prepare it for service.

"You Are God's Field" (1 Corinthians 3:5–9)

1. Paul plants the seed, Apollos waters it, and God makes it grow **(v. 6).** In other words, God had called Paul to evangelize the Corinthians, to attend their birth into God's kingdom by proclaiming the Gospel to them in such a way that they believed it and became Christians. God had called Apollos to nurture the Corinthians in their faith, to attend to their growth and development in faith and Christian living. In the case of both Paul and Apollos, God was working and was responsible for the outcome—even as He is today.

2. The purpose of the tasks assigned by God is that people come to saving faith as the Corinthians did and remain in that faith until God receives them into His eternal kingdom of glory in heaven. While God used Paul and Apollos to accomplish this task, God Himself brought it about through the Gospel.

3. While being called by God to have a part in the work of His kingdom of grace is a wonderful privilege in itself, God in His gracious love promises to bless the work of those who serve faithfully and steadfastly and to give them additional opportunities through which He will bless them, as the master does in Jesus' parable.

Jesus Christ, the Foundation (1 Corinthians 3:10–15)

1. Christ provides the solid foundation for the church since He is the solid rock upon which Christians stand through the storms of this life. His Word and His promises are rock-solid and reliable in life and death because He is forever faithful.

2. While Paul correctly understood the vital nature of his work as an apostle and upheld its importance and effect, he also knew that it was God's grace that accomplished its great work through him. Paul viewed

himself only as Christ's instrument, with Christ Himself responsible for results.

3. We today also are to be concerned that we use the solid and enduring building materials God Himself provides for building the church—the Gospel by which the Holy Spirit works and builds up the church. The "means of grace" (Word and sacraments) are the channel by which we receive God's power. Christian teaching grounded in these means of grace results in committed lives and faithful living. The worthless materials include teaching based on human ideas. This kind of teaching results in unbelief and uncommitted lives.

You Are God's Temple (1 Corinthians 3:16–23)

1. Viewing the church as sacred, as under God's protection, and as the place where the Holy Spirit works will encourage us to think of the church as God's kingdom, as a spiritual reality, and as God's work instead of thinking of the church as a collection of sinful people, often with self-centered goals.

2. Paul says that Apollos, Cephas, Paul, and all else belong to all the believers (v. 22). Christ has not divided up His spiritual blessings or kingdom but has given all of them to all of us in common. All believers belong to Christ; He is our Lord. And Christ Himself, according to His human nature, belongs to God. God has left no room for factions; God has given His kingdom in its entirety to Christians, and all Christians belong altogether to God.

The Word for Us

1. Encourage the class to share their personal struggles and victories of faith. Do not embarrass anyone by calling on them but let volunteers respond.

2. Try to get beyond tasks and offices in the church to that of witness and service to specific people and in specific situations by praying for them, encouraging them, or assisting them in various ways. Focus on the fact that God's Word works and that we need not feel discouraged if we do not see immediate results.

3. We also are to be concerned that we use the Gospel to build up our own lives in Christ and that we then devote these lives to God's kingdom. Don't force anyone to answer.

Closing

Sing or pray together the hymn stanzas printed in the Study Guide. Ask participants for prayer concerns or requests. Pray or have a volunteer pray for those things identified by the participants.

Lesson 4

Spiritual Leadership
(1 Corinthians 4:1–21)

Theme Verse

Invite a volunteer to read the theme verse for this lesson.

Goal

Read aloud the goal statement.

What's Going On Here?

Read aloud or have a volunteer read aloud this introductory section.

Searching the Scriptures

Read aloud or have volunteers read aloud the portions of Scripture before discussing the questions.

Servants and Stewards (1 Corinthians 4:1–7)

1. The Holy Spirit reveals God's mysteries to us through the Holy Scriptures, written by inspired prophets, evangelists, and apostles.

2. The primary requirement of a minister is to be faithful as a steward of the Gospel. (a) Certainly a minister is accountable to the congregation for carrying out the work of the ministry diligently, competently, and in keeping with God's commands. As Bereans checked out Paul's teachings with the Bible, so congregations today use the Scriptures to check out the teaching and leadership they receive from their pastors. (b) God expects pastors to be decent, law-abiding citizens of their community. A minister who transgresses the law faces the same penalty others face, and a minister who fails to live a moral life faces public disapproval and scorn. (c) A minister has his own conscience and self-respect to satisfy. (d) None of these matter in the face of God's own judgment of a minister's faithfulness. Congregation, community, and self may all be wrong in their judgment, but God is never wrong in His judgment.

Proud Critics but Humble Apostles (1 Corinthians 4:8–13)

1. When Paul says, "How I wish that you really had become kings," he implies that they were acting in an arrogant manner. They were not displaying Christian humility or the desire to serve but were proud and overbearing. Paul is using irony and sarcasm (Law) to lead them to repentance.

2. Paul recalls many hardships and sufferings for the cause of the

Gospel, including imprisonment, floggings and beatings, stoning, and shipwreck.

3. From these and similar experiences, Paul learned to know his own weakness and limitations. He also learned that through the gracious work of Christ he could accomplish much.

Fatherly Admonitions (1 Corinthians 4:14–21)

1. Paul set an example for the Corinthians by living the lifestyle he taught. His own conduct and manner of life supported and affirmed his teaching.

2. Paul calls Timothy, his young companion and co-worker, "my son" because Paul had led Timothy to know Christ. Timothy became Paul's close friend and co-worker. Because of this and also their age difference, Paul knew that Timothy thought of him as his father.

3. We do not and cannot know what lies before us in the future, but God knows. And we know that God loves us and will bring us one day into His heavenly kingdom, where we will share His glory with Him. Therefore, we willingly entrust our future into the keeping of our gracious and loving God, who will cause every circumstance of life to bring about eternal good for us.

The Word for Us

1. Many duties, responsibilities, and qualifications of ministers are provided in Paul's letters to Timothy and to Titus, as well as in other portions of the New Testament. In **1 Timothy 4:11–16,** Paul writes of the minister's duty to teach God's Word, set a Christian example for others, and diligently do the tasks of the ministry in public and private.

2. Certainly Christians are suffering persecution and hardship for the sake of Christ in many parts of the world. Perhaps participants even know personally Christians who are enduring a hard time at home, at work, or elsewhere because of their faith and loyalty to Christ. We can pray for persecuted Christians everywhere and help them as God gives opportunity to do so.

3. Jesus encouraged His disciples to respond to persecution with faith, rejoicing, and love. When we are called upon to suffer disapproval or hardship in any way for Christ's sake, we also can ask God to enable us to respond with cheerfulness, faith, and love.

4. Love desires the good of those who are loved. Love tells the truth, even when the truth is not comfortable or easy. While love prefers to deal with others gently, sternness is sometimes the truest expression of love. Encourage participants to talk about this.

Closing

Sing or pray together the closing hymn. Speak a brief prayer, perhaps asking God to bless and guide the spiritual leaders of the congregation to which the participants belong. Also ask God to bless the way all members of the congregation work together.

Lesson 5

Potential for Regression
(1 Corinthians 5:1–13)

Theme Verse

Invite a volunteer to read the theme verse for this lesson.

Goal

Read aloud the goal statement.

What's Going On Here?

Read aloud or have a volunteer read aloud this introductory section.

Searching the Scriptures

Read aloud or have volunteers read aloud the portions of Scripture before discussing the questions.

A Grave Public Scandal (1 Corinthians 5:1–5)

1. **Leviticus 18:8** and **17** call this sin wicked. Incest destroys both individuals and families. The great harm done by the sin of incest (usually perpetrated by a parent rather than a child) is evident in the severe, long-lasting problems experienced by its victims.

2. **Deuteronomy 27:20** pronounces those guilty of incest "cursed," and **Leviticus 18:29** demands that those who commit this and other similar sins be "cut off from [God's] people." This meant that the person found himself/herself under divine judgment. It also referred to banishment or to execution. Similarly, Paul calls for the man who had taken his father's wife to be put out of the Christian fellowship and handed over to Satan **(v. 5)**. Paul intends, not the eternal damnation of the sinner but that as he experiences the consequences of life outside the kingdom of light, he will by

God's grace come to repentance.

The Lesson of the Leaven (1 Corinthians 5:6–13)

1. Accept reasonable responses from volunteers. If they use personal experiences, ask that they not name the individuals involved in their stories.

2. Paul refers to Christ as our Passover Lamb because he saw Jesus the same way John the Baptizer did when he called Christ "the Lamb of God, who takes away the sin of the world." Jesus came into this world to be an atoning sacrifice that removes our sins and thus clears the way for restoration of fellowship between us and our God. Just as the Passover lamb was sacrificed and its blood on the doorpost protected those in the household from the angel of death, so the blood of Jesus, who was slain on Calvary's cross, saves us from the eternal punishment we deserve for our sins (**John 1:29**).

3. The Christian who deals with a sinning brother or sister will show a humble and gentle spirit, as befits those who know they themselves are not without fault and who know they also are prone to fall into sin. Such a Christian will seek to win an erring brother or sister, not self-righteously or with a superior attitude, but as one forgiven sinner seeking to share God's grace with another sinner.

The Word for Us

1. Jesus' purpose is to save sinners, not to oversee their condemnation. Jesus will be present with us to guide us as we work with unrepentant sinners. Led by Christ, we will seek to restore sinners by helping them to cease behavior that is un-Christian and that destroys Christian fellowship.

2. We cannot altogether avoid associating with sinners. We must continue to earn a living and carry out the common responsibilities of life. However, in our minds, we are to make a clear distinction between God's kingdom and the devil's kingdom. We are to remember that we belong to God's kingdom, not to the world system around us.

3. Paul distinguishes between those inside the church and those outside of it. It is not a Christian's business to judge unbelievers. God will do that. This frees us to concentrate on presenting God's saving Gospel to sinners instead of on judging them. While we are aware of the sins we see going on around us, and while we cannot approve of such sins, we will focus our energies on saving sinners and let God be the Judge of those who refuse to repent. But believers **do** judge other believers in the case of open and known sins (**vv. 12–13**). Jesus makes it clear, however, that this detecting and dealing with sin is to begin in our own hearts. We are first to see our

own sins and failings. Then, having honestly and earnestly confessed our own sins and received God's gracious forgiveness, we will be better able to deal with the sins of others.

Closing

Pray together the prayer printed in the Study Guide.

Lesson 6

Moral Regression
(1 Corinthians 6:1–20)

Theme Verse

Invite a volunteer to read the theme verse for this lesson.

Goal

Read aloud the goal statement.

What's Going On Here?

Read aloud or have a volunteer read aloud this introductory section.

Searching the Scriptures

Read aloud or have volunteers read aloud the portions of Scripture before discussing the questions.

Christians Going to Court (1 Corinthians 6:1–8)

1. What Paul says to the Corinthians is not to be understood as disparaging the usefulness of government for Christians or the legitimacy of government as an institution established by God. Paul told the Roman congregation that Christians should submit to the secular authorities, even though they were pagan, since the government is "God's servant," an agent of God's wrath to bring judgment on the wrongdoer.

2. Believers will have a part in judging the evil angels who rebelled against God and followed Satan. The Bible also refers to these disobedient and wicked angels as devils or demons.

3. Rather than respond with hatred and retaliation, Paul suggests that Christians should allow themselves to be wronged and even cheated.

Encourage volunteers to share their responses. If time allows, ask how they react to this idea.

Out of the Mire of Pagan Vices (1 Corinthians 6:9–11)

1. The composite list will be a long one. It would contain, from **1 Corinthians 6:9–10,** the sexually immoral, idolaters, adulterers, male prostitutes, homosexual offenders, thieves, the greedy, drunkards, slanderers, and swindlers. **Galatians 5:19–21** would add those guilty of impurity, debauchery, witchcraft, hatred, discord, jealousy, fits of rage, selfish ambition, dissension, factions, envy, and orgies.

2. In a way, the death penalty for sin still stands. Sin still results in death—eternal death.

3. The good news is that God laid all of our sins on Jesus **(Isaiah 53:4–6),** who paid this penalty for sin on our behalf and in our place **(1 Corinthians 15:3).** As a result, God no longer counts our sins against us. We are reconciled to God for the sake of Christ. In Jesus we are God's new creation **(2 Corinthians 5:17–18).**

God's Claim on Our Bodies (1 Corinthians 6:12–20)

1. Although permissible, some things are not beneficial or constructive. Some permissible behaviors may lead to sin or to addiction, for example. Participants may cite smoking, for instance, or, in some cases, drinking alcoholic beverages.

2. By raising the physical body of Jesus from the dead and promising to raise our bodies, God shows the high value He places on the body.

3. The Holy Spirit dwells within believers. The place where God dwells is a temple. The bodies of believers are holy places, and the use of our bodies in a dishonorable way constitutes sacrilege, the profaning of a holy place, and is insulting to the Lord. We honor God with the body by using it for His purposes and to bring glory and honor to Him by obeying His will.

4. In **Romans 6:13,** Paul tells us to offer the parts of our bodies to God for His use as instruments of righteousness. We use our bodies as instruments of righteousness when we use them to worship and pray, to speak the Gospel to others, to serve others in their needs, and to do God's work.

The Word for Us

1. By resolving disputes among themselves, Christians have the opportunity to use such Gospel-based actions as forgiveness, forbearance, yielding to others for the sake of peace, and love. Civil courts, on the other hand, are limited to such law-based actions as strict justice, punishment, and restitution.

2. We as individuals and as a church rejoice that God has washed away

homosexual sins as well as other sins. We must identify homosexual behavior as sinful, not as an alternative, acceptable lifestyle. But we can accept the person who has homosexual desires as one loved and forgiven by God.

3. Jesus gave up His life to secure our redemption. Our bodies, then, belong to God, since He paid such a high price for them. To take what belongs to God and use it in a way He has not authorized is to rob God of His property.

Closing

Sing or pray the closing hymn. Ask participants for prayer concerns or requests. Pray or have a volunteer pray for those things identified by the participants.

Lesson 7

To Marry or Not to Marry?
(1 Corinthians 7:1–40)

Theme Verse

Invite a volunteer to read the theme verse for this lesson.

Goal

Read aloud the goal statement. Point out that the goal will briefly describe the direction the lesson will take.

What's Going On Here?

Read aloud or have a volunteer read aloud this introductory section.

Searching the Scriptures

Read aloud or have volunteers read aloud the portions of Scripture before discussing the questions.

It Is Good Not to Marry If ... (1 Corinthians 7:1–9)

1. Paul counsels younger widows to marry so that the church would not have to support them and they would not become busybodies (**1 Timothy 5:14**). From this verse, which counsels widows to marry, we see that Paul

did not discourage marriage as such but gave his counsel to marry or not to marry in light of other circumstances.

2. Paul recommends marriage because of the temptation to immorality **(v. 2)**. Our fallen human nature is all too prone to satisfy sexual desire through sinful relationships, as well as to use sex to satisfy a self-centered desire to dominate and use other people.

3. Because husband and wife become one flesh in marriage, they belong to each other. Not only their own needs and desires but also the needs and desires of the spouse are to be considered in the sexual side of their marriage relationship.

4. Sometimes it may seem a couple would be better off if they waited a while before marrying. Many couples would be well advised to finish a college education, fulfill military obligations, or gain more maturity before taking on the responsibilities of marriage. But despite such factors, some couples will not be deterred. It may be wiser to accede than attempt to block their wishes. In cases like these, friends and family can look for ways to help the couple have a successful marriage.

Counsel to the Married (1 Corinthians 7:10–16)

1. Paul calls on Christians who separate or divorce to remain unmarried. Such a course would acknowledge the lifelong intention of the marriage commitment and remove an impediment to a future reconciliation.

Deal with this question sensitively! Your group will likely include one or more believers who have been through a divorce. Perhaps some have remarried. Paul here affirms the biblical principle of marriage—one man, one woman, for life. This ideal goes back to Eden, and it originated in God's heart of love for His people. Anyone who has lived through the breakup of a marriage knows something of the suffering He wanted to spare us. On the other hand, we live in a fallen world with sin in our hearts and in the hearts of those around us. Paul himself hints at the possibility of divorce in **verse 13**. At times, husbands and wives desert their spouses—either by actually walking out or through physical, emotional, or spiritual abuse. In a case like this, **verse 15** applies—the believer is not bound.

2. The purposes of marriage are (a) sexual fulfillment within a committed, loving, and self-giving relationship; (b) providing a nurturing climate in which children may be born and brought up; and (c) companionship and help throughout life.

Accepting Life on Its Own Terms (1 Corinthians 7:17–24)

1. Gentile Christians, as well as Jews, are saved through faith in Jesus Christ, who fulfilled the Old Testament ceremonial law and thus abolished it. Gentile Christians who allow themselves to be forced into circumcision

are removing themselves from God's grace as their all-sufficient way of salvation and are placing themselves under the obligation to keep the entire ceremonial law. Now that the Savior has come and is received by all peoples through faith, circumcision has lost its crucial value as a sign of one's relationship with God. God has reconciled each person, whether Jew or Gentile, to Himself in Christ.

2. If a slave could become free, Paul urged him to do so. We belong to the Lord, not to other people. Paul regarded slavery as contrary to the peace God has brought about through Christ's work. Human slavery is totally at odds with God's view of human beings.

Counsel to the Unmarried (1 Corinthians 7:25–35)

1. Paul gives as his reasons for advising the Corinthian virgins to remain unmarried "the present crisis," the desire to spare them "many troubles," and freedom from having to make a choice between concern for the Lord's affairs and concern for husband and family. In a similar situation these reasons would certainly be as valid today as they were then. Christians will want to weigh how they will best be able to serve God in their individual circumstances.

2. Paul urges a sense of perspective based on an understanding that our circumstances in this world are temporary; eternal things matter most. Both the problems and the pleasures that have their base in this world need to be kept in that perspective.

A Word for the Engaged and Widows (1 Corinthians 7:36–40)

1. Paul suggests that a person considering marriage work through the decision thoughtfully and avoid caving in to pressure. This remains good advice for young people today. Deciding to marry ought to be a thoughtful choice, freely made. No one should be pressured into marriage or marry when they are unsure about it.

2. Responses to this question may vary according to the age and situation of the participants.

The Word for Us

1. Being single is an acceptable lifestyle according to Scripture. In fact, it may have special advantages that lead a Christian to choose it, if personal gifts permit. By remaining unmarried, a Christian will have more time to devote to Christian service. In periods of persecution, a Christian may not wish to expose a spouse or children to deprivation and suffering. Members of your study group may think of other reasons to remain single.

2. Ask for ideas from your group. If some members of your study group are single, they may have particular observations to make or suggestions

to offer about ways the congregation can serve and include single adults who never married or those who are divorced or widowed. Unintentionally, congregations sometimes exclude single adults or apply a subtle pressure to marry. Move the group beyond the idea of Bible studies and recreation planned for singles. Encourage them to think through occasions, such as holidays, moving, and hospitalizations, that present singles with special challenges.

3. Paul advises Christians to choose marriage partners who are also believers in the Lord. Christian marriage partners can encourage and strengthen one another in faith and life. An unbelieving partner's influence may be negative and discouraging. Marrying an unbeliever with the hope of converting that person, though a real possibility, is by no means certain and can be a risky way to do mission work. It may result not in the addition of someone to God's kingdom but the subtraction of the person who went into the marriage as a Christian.

4. They were assigned their place in life by God, or Paul says they were "called" to their situation **(vv. 17, 24).** We may see God leading us in our lives. While God has given us the freedom to make choices regarding such things as marriage and vocation, we also can be sure that God's will is operative in our life situations. When we remember that God loves us and desires to use all of our circumstances for His glory, we may take up our vocation and place in life with confidence and enthusiasm.

5. Paul urges a sense of perspective based on an understanding that our circumstances in this world are temporary; eternal things matter most. Both the problems and the pleasures that have their base in this world need to be kept in that perspective.

Closing

Sing or pray together the closing hymn. Ask participants for prayer concerns or requests. Pray or have a volunteer pray for those things identified by the participants.

Lesson 8
Christian Freedom
(1 Corinthians 8:1–13)

Theme Verse
Invite a volunteer to read the theme verse for this lesson.

Goal
Read aloud the goal statement. Point out that the goal will briefly describe the direction the lesson will take.

What's Going On Here?
Read aloud or have a volunteer read aloud this introductory section.

Searching the Scriptures
Read aloud or have volunteers read aloud portions of Scripture before discussing the questions.

"Knowledge" and Love (1 Corinthians 8:1–6)
1. Simply to know facts about God is not enough. After all, the devil knows the facts. But he does not trust in God—and that is what is required for salvation. Faith is more than an experience of the intellect; it is an attitude of the heart.

2. When someone simply "knows" but has no faith in God, this person's knowledge not only does no good, it may even become a problem. This kind of knowledge "puffs up"; it may cause pride, which acts lovelessly. We may even begin to imagine we have no need for Jesus and for His salvation. The person who loves God is known by God **(v. 3),** and this love "builds up" **(v. 1).** It builds up the individual, who is then motivated to build up others.

3. Idolatry is far more widespread than we realize. Those who worship the gods and goddesses of Hinduism, for example, are found around the world, as are other religions in which people bow down to idols of gold and silver. However, the most prominent idol is the self. God alone knows how many sins are committed in the service of this idol.

Love to the Weak in Faith (1 Corinthians 8:7–13)
1. Christians still under the delusion that idol gods really do exist would be confused when they observed other Christians, who professed loyalty to Christ, having contact with an idol god by eating meat sacrificed to that

idol. They might conclude that one could worship the triune God and other gods at the same time (the belief of most pagans), or they might think that other Christians really did not have the true faith they claimed to have. Encourage participants to share their comments.

2. Not only may we offend or destroy the faith of a weaker Christian by disregarding that Christian's conscience and feelings, but by harming another Christian in this way we also sin against Christ Himself, who died to save that weaker Christian. Encourage participants to comment on sensitivity to the feelings of weaker Christians.

The Word for Us

1. Both God the Father and Jesus Christ (God the Son) are equally God. All things came to be through them and both are to be worshiped as God. (Of course the same is true of the Holy Spirit, although that truth is not stated in these verses.)

2. Encourage participants to comment.

3. Anyone who is stronger is obliged to assist someone who is not as strong. This also applies to faith in Christ. The stronger Christian will want to do what builds up another Christian who is not as strong; the stronger Christian will certainly not do things that injure or discourage a weaker Christian—that would be unloving.

Closing

Sing or pray together the closing hymn printed in the Study Guide. Ask participants for prayer concerns or requests. Pray or have a volunteer pray for those things identified by the participants.

Lesson 9

Your Rights and the Needs of Others
(1 Corinthians 9:1–27)

Theme Verses

Invite a volunteer to read the theme verses for this lesson.

Goal

Read aloud the goal statement. Point out that the goal will briefly describe the direction the lesson will take.

What's Going On Here?

Read aloud or have a volunteer read aloud this introductory section.

Searching the Scriptures

Read aloud or have volunteers read aloud the suggested portions of Scripture before discussing the questions.

Rights of a Duly Called Apostle (1 Corinthians 9:1–12a, 13–14)

1. Paul was not one of the Twelve whom Jesus had called during His ministry before His crucifixion and resurrection. Paul had not followed Jesus during those years as the other apostles had. Nevertheless, Paul had been called as an apostle by Jesus directly and personally when, on the road to Damascus, as Paul was going to arrest Christians there, a blinding light struck him to the ground. Paul received Christ's commission to serve as His ambassador.

2. The fact that the Spirit used the preaching of Paul to bring people to faith and to form a congregation is proof of his apostleship. Through this activity and in the results He brought about, God the Holy Spirit had imprinted His presence and authority on the work of Paul as an apostle.

3. Paul says that he was not inferior to the "super apostles" even though he says, "I am nothing." It is typical of Paul to magnify his God-given office but to minimize himself personally.

4. The first right that Paul maintains is the right to a living from his work. The church has the responsibility of supporting Gospel workers with food and drink and other physical needs. The second right is the right to marry. While Paul had the gift of being able to remain unmarried, other apostles (for example, Peter) were married.

Rights Sacrificed for the Gospel (1 Corinthians 9:12b, 15–18)

1. Out of love for the congregation Paul did not claim his right of support. Also, Paul was particularly conscious of the grace of God that had come to him contrary to all expectation or deserving, and he desired to give the Gospel as freely as he himself had received it. His reward was that he could offer the Gospel without charge. In addition, he avoided the charge that he was doing what he did "only for the money" or as another in a long line of religious frauds whose only motive was to "fleece the sheep."

2. Paul knew that he was God's special, chosen instrument to preach the Gospel, especially to the Gentiles. He had been personally called, appointed, and commissioned. While Paul knew that he had in no way deserved such a special status, he also knew that God had chosen him uniquely and particularly. Therefore, he had no choice.

3. While most pastors and other professional church workers earn their

living entirely from their work, some engage in "worker/priest" ministries in which they earn at least the major portion of their income in some non-church vocation or job and serve a small or very poor congregation on a part-time basis for little or no pay. These ministries are unusual and extra-ordinary (except in some Baptist, Pentecostal, or fundamentalist denominations). But they do exist and serve a genuine need in some cases.

Rights Sacrificed to Attain the Goal (1 Corinthians 9:19–27)

1. Paul is free of any claims of others upon him. He serves his Lord and is answerable to Him for everything. Also, Paul is free from having to fulfill the obligations of the Law (impossible for our sinful human nature) because of the grace we receive through Jesus.

2. While Paul is not obligated to serve others to earn his salvation, he willingly serves because of his thankfulness to the Lord and his desire to respond to the Lord's call to serve others as the Lord Himself became our servant. Paul serves not under unwilling compulsion but with a willing love.

The Word for Us

1. Church workers today have the right to marry and to receive a livelihood from the service they provide within the church.

2. Participants will identify many blessings they enjoy from the Gospel. The blessings of the Gospel include both the blessing that we ourselves enjoy salvation through Christ and also the joy that we are able to share the good news of salvation and its blessings with others.

3. When Paul was with the Jews, he respected their traditions in order to be accepted. He did so without compromising his faith in order to get a hearing for the Gospel. When he was with the weak he dealt with them gently and with understanding, so he might win and strengthen them in their faith in Jesus. Encourage group members to specify strategies they might adopt to win the mission targets they have identified.

Closing

Sing or pray together the closing hymn. Ask participants for prayer concerns or requests. Pray or have a volunteer pray for those things identified by the participants.

Lesson 10

Taking Temptation Seriously
(1 Corinthians 10:1–33)

Theme Verse

Invite a volunteer to read the theme verse for this lesson.

Goal

Read aloud the goal statement.

What's Going On Here?

Read aloud or have a volunteer read aloud this introductory section.

Searching the Scriptures

Read aloud or have volunteers read aloud the portions of Scripture before discussing the questions.

People of Israel Not Immune to Idolatry (1 Corinthians 10:1–13)

1. Invite volunteers to comment on the Old Testament events to which Paul refers. Was anything they read new or surprising to them?

2. The Israelites became idolaters when they worshiped the golden calf **(v. 7)**. The Israelites committed sexual immorality with the Moabite women at Peor **(v. 8)**. The Israelites tested the Lord at Rephidim when they quarreled with Moses because they had no water **(v. 9)**. God destroyed 250 of the people of the families of Korah, Dathan, and Abiram. Their sin was grumbling and insolence **(v. 10)**.

Corinthians Shun Idolatry (1 Corinthians 10:14–22)

1. How marvelous that in the Lord's Supper we enjoy intimate fellowship with our Lord as He gives His body and blood—the same body and blood given and shed for our salvation on the cross. How awful then to join ourselves also with demons through any kind of idolatry.

2. Paul refers to this common loaf made up of many pieces to remind the Corinthians that the Lord has made us one church through our common participation in Christ. By sharing in the Lord's Supper together we express and participate in our unity in the body of Christ.

3. The sacrifices of pagans were offered to demons **(v. 20)**. How could anyone possibly think of worshiping Satan and the Lord Jesus at the same time, by worshiping both at pagan temples and at God's altar **(v. 21)**?

Seeking the Good of Others (1 Corinthians 10:23–33)

1. The criteria Paul repeats is that our action must be "beneficial" and "constructive" for others. To attempt to do what is beneficial and constructive for others and not to think only of ourselves is following the principle of Christian love.

2. The "law of Christ" asks that we do what will benefit others. It asks that we help shoulder the burdens others carry. In this way we will be like Christ, who did not come into this world for Himself but for us and our needs. Note that this does not always involve "being nice." Christian love is sometimes tough. We speak the truth, in love, with the other person's well-being as our goal.

3. Christians can, in good conscience, eat meat offered to idols and sold at the market since the meat belongs to the Lord; He has provided it. We may receive all of the gifts that come to us from God's hand with thanksgiving—that is, recognizing and acknowledging that they come from Him. However, if someone with whom we're sharing a meal points out that the meat was connected to an idol when it was used in a sacrifice, then, Paul says, do not eat it.

The Word for Us

1. We can fall. But God will not allow us to be tempted beyond our ability to handle the temptation and will always provide a way of escape because He is faithful. Encourage participants to express what this means to them personally.

2. Anything or anyone who is more important to us than God is our idol. With that understanding, we can easily see that we often commit idolatry.

3. Encourage participants to suggest effective ways to flee from this temptation. For example, by drawing strength from God's Word as they read and study the Scriptures, as they worship with other believers, as they pray for strength, as they receive the Lord's Supper, and through the encouragement of Christian family and friends. Accept other reasonable responses.

4. When we intend to come to the Lord's Supper, we need first to prepare ourselves by asking God the Holy Spirit to help us examine our lives to find the sins we may be harboring there. Then we need to ask God for forgiveness in Jesus and for His strength to turn from these sins and toward a more Christlike life.

5. We eat and drink to the glory of God by being thankful to God for life and its sustenance and by seeking to serve God and other people with the strength He provides.

Closing

Sing or speak together the closing hymn. Ask participants for prayer concerns or requests. Pray or have a volunteer pray for those things identified by the participants.

Lesson 11

The Lord's Supper with Reverence
(1 Corinthians 11:1–34)

Theme Verse

Invite a volunteer to read the theme verse for this lesson.

Goal

Read aloud the goal statement.

What's Going On Here?

Read aloud or have a volunteer read aloud this introductory section.

Searching the Scriptures

Read aloud or have volunteers read aloud the portions of Scripture before discussing the questions.

Women and Men at Worship (1 Corinthians 11:2–16)

1. Paul is willing to become all things to all people in order to save some. He looked at others with a servant's heart. Jesus did not come to be served but to serve everyone else by giving His life as a ransom from sin, death, and the devil.

2. Paul is concerned that God's people uphold and maintain the will of God expressed in creation. This includes the order and structure that God has built into marriage and family life.

3. According to the order of creation, men and women have separate roles reflected in certain ways of relating to each other, especially in the church and in marriage. In the order of salvation, however, no distinction separates men from women (nor people in any other way). All such distinctions disappear in regard to our place in God's kingdom of grace.

The Love Feast (1 Corinthians 11:17–26)

1. Paul admonishes the Corinthians for creating divisions within the church and for despising and humiliating some of the believers.

2. The church at Corinth met in halls or homes to worship and celebrate the Lord's Supper. The early Christians customarily shared a fellowship meal, which they called a "love feast." Paul denies that the Corinthians are observing the Lord's Supper since their selfish behavior contradicted the very nature of the Lord's Supper **(vv. 20–21)**. Some members of the congregation did not wait for others but went ahead and ate by themselves. Some had more food than they needed and stuffed themselves, while some did not have enough. Some drank themselves into a stupor. How very opposite from the kind of behavior we might expect from Christians who have shared in the assurance of the Lord's Supper that the Savior had given His body and shed His blood for us all and has united us in Him in the family of God.

Admonition to Communicants (1 Corinthians 11:27–34)

1. In examining ourselves we want to remember that we are sinners who need the forgiveness Christ offers to us in the Lord's Supper. We also will remind ourselves of the promises Christ has made in connection with the Holy Supper, and we will ask ourselves whether or not we believe those promises. Accept other reasonable responses. "That person is truly worthy and well prepared who has faith in these words: 'Given and shed for you for the forgiveness of sins' " (Luther's Small Catechism, 1986 translation, p. 29).

2. Encourage participants to comment on methods of preparation they have personally found helpful. Share your own thoughts as time permits.

The Word for Us

1. Point out that in New Testament times, Jewish people of both genders covered their heads when they worshiped. In Gentile cultures, men uncovered their heads to show respect and submission. Gentile women, however, who appeared in public with their heads uncovered expressed disregard or even contempt for standards of modesty and even morality. A woman whose head was shaved was either in public disgrace or openly rebelling against social customs regarding the role of women. While the customs that define modesty will change somewhat from one culture to another, Christians will desire to uphold the customs that apply so that God's name is not brought into disrepute. Certainly, also, Christians will want to live out the moral standards God has given us in Scripture.

2. How often to celebrate the Lord's Supper is left to the decision of

each Christian congregation and to individual members. But certainly when we understand and value what Christ offers us in His Supper we will want to commune often.

Closing

Sing or speak together the closing hymn. Ask participants for prayer concerns or requests. Pray or have a volunteer pray for those things identified by the participants.

Lesson 12

Spiritual Gifts
(1 Corinthians 12–13)

Theme Verse

Invite a volunteer to read the theme verse for this lesson.

Goal

Read aloud the goal statement.

What's Going On Here?

Read aloud or have a volunteer read aloud this introductory section.

Searching the Scriptures

Read aloud or have volunteers read aloud the portions of Scripture before discussing the questions.

Faith and Other Gifts of the Spirit (1 Corinthians 12:1–11)

1. Paul makes it clear that the same Spirit who gives us saving faith also gifts believers with specific abilities for the good of the church. We did not earn or deserve these any more than we earned or deserved the gift of saving faith.

2. In grace, God has chosen who will receive which gifts. Not all Christians have the same gifts, but all believers are gifted.

3. God's wisdom ("secret," since it is not evident to mere human intelligence) centers in Jesus Christ, our Savior, and in His cross. The gift of wisdom may refer to sharing this wisdom with others in winsome ways or it

may refer to the ability to apply the truths of the Gospel in specific situations in the lives of others.

The Human Body: Example of a Coordinated Whole (1 Corinthians 12:12–20)

1. God has arranged each organ of the human body to serve the whole body in a way no other organ can. So it is with us as members of Christ's body, the church. Our spiritual gifts may differ from those of other members, but all of us need one another. Christ's body is complete and functions at less than capacity when even one member is damaged, missing, or not performing as God planned.

2. When one of our brothers or sisters in Christ experiences grief or pain, we grieve with them. On the other hand, when someone experiences success or triumph, we celebrate, too. When one member of the group is sick, we are there at the bedside to lend encouragement, to help, and to comfort. When one is insulted or mistreated, other members of the group become angry, too. In these ways we show Christlike love and care.

3. Some spiritual gifts are more critical to the extension of Christ's kingdom than others. But Jesus makes it clear that those who humbly serve others, as He Himself humbly served us, are great in God's kingdom. Not our gifts, but our spirit of service, makes us great in the kingdom of heaven.

The Qualities of Christian Love (1 Corinthians 13:1–13)

1. In **1 Corinthians 12:31b** Paul says that love is "the most excellent way" to use our spiritual gifts. The love that God's Spirit brings about in our lives gives meaning and value to the ways in which we use our spiritual gifts. Without that, we're just making noise **(v. 1)**.

2. The love Paul describes—love that comes from God and is like God—is not focused on itself but on others.

3. Being known by God as we live in a personal relationship with Him is essential to knowing the truth about God. Without the Spirit's presence in their hearts, people cannot understand the truths of God's grace and saving will at all.

The Word for Us

1. Paul tells us that the Holy Spirit enables us to believe in Jesus and to acknowledge Him as our Lord.

2. The believers in Corinth apparently were abusing their spiritual gifts and so can we. Most often the cause is spiritual pride. Jealousy and judgmental attitudes also can create problems.

3. Let participants comment on what they are looking forward to seeing

or knowing when they are made perfect in heaven.

4. Love is the greatest of the trio because God Himself is love. Love will continue eternally.

Closing

Sing or speak together the closing hymn. Ask participants for prayer concerns or requests. Pray or have a volunteer pray for those things identified by the participants.

Lesson 13

Meaningful Worship
(1 Corinthians 14:1–40)

Theme Verse

Invite a volunteer to read the theme verse for this lesson.

Goal

Read aloud the goal statement. Point out that the goal will briefly describe the direction the lesson will take.

What's Going On Here?

Read aloud or have a volunteer read aloud this introductory section.

Searching the Scriptures

Read aloud or have volunteers read aloud the portions of Scripture before discussing the questions.

Mere Sounds Do Not Edify the Church (1 Corinthians 14:1–13)

1. Prophecy builds up the church, strengthens us individually and corporately. As necessary, remind participants how the Scriptures use the term *prophecy*. Sometimes it refers to foretelling events that have not yet occurred. More often, though, it refers to "forth-telling," proclaiming the Word of the Lord.

2. While Paul did not forbid speaking in tongues in the public worship service **(14:39),** he did strictly regulate the use of this gift in public worship and subordinated it to prophecy since prophecy had the potential of

building up the church while tongues that were uninterpreted did not. Paul gives priority in the worship service to communicating Law and Gospel in words everyone could understand.

3. Paul wants to correct two abuses of tongues: (1) disorder in worship service caused by some who were exercising this gift **(chapter 14),** and (2) spiritual pride in the hearts of some who thought they were better or more spiritual than other Christians because they had the gift **(chapter 12).**

Praying with Spirit and Mind (1 Corinthians 14:14–21)

1. We worship the Lord with our intellect and with our spirit. Jesus once summarized the First Table of the Law in these words: Love the Lord your God with all your heart and with all your soul and with all your mind. Our Lord wants every part of our being to worship Him.

2. While we know from Scripture that infants and children share the sinful nature common to all humans **(Psalm 51:5),** they are relatively inexperienced in practicing evil. Paul means that we are not to become experienced in committing evil.

3. On the other hand, when it comes to doing—conforming our lives to God's will—especially in the way we value and use our spiritual gifts, our Lord wants us to have as much practice and experience as possible.

Let Order Prevail (1 Corinthians 14:22–33)

1. If unbelievers or inquirers should be present at Christian worship where things were said in an unintelligible language, such a visitor would obviously receive no benefit from that part of the service. Such an experience might even alienate the visitor and turn the visitor against Christ or against Christian worship.

2. We see Paul's principle at work in the matter of speaking in tongues. Paul allows it, provided it is done in an orderly manner, there is no confusion, and *when someone can interpret what is being said in the language.* When this cannot be done, the church is not strengthened, and Paul directs that it be omitted.

3. Paul insisted on an orderly use of both tongues and prophecy in public worship. Whatever form of worship is used, however informal or spontaneous, everyone present ought to be able to understand and benefit.

Paul's Instruction by Divine Authority (1 Corinthians 14:34–40)

1. When a Christian voluntarily submits herself to the Lord's will for her participation in marriage and in the church, this demonstrates her desire to be God's servant and her faith in His plan for her. A respectful reserve in public worship is fitting for a woman who has trustfully placed herself

under God's will. Far from demeaning or devaluing her, such an attitude exhibits an inner strength and self-control.

2. Not only Christian women show their faith and love for God by their attitude toward men, but Christian men show the same kind of faith and love for God when they treat women with respect and honor. Christian men who follow God's will in regard to their relationship with women will not domineer but will treat women, beginning with their own wives, with deep courtesy and respect. Such an attitude shows their love for God and a desire to imitate Him in the way He treats His people.

The Word for Us

1. The words imply that God is eager to answer prayers for the good of the whole church. If an individual Christian or a congregation perceives a need, that person or congregation may pray that God would provide help. Moreover, God's help might come through the person(s) who prayed. Paul's words emphasize that gifts are always given to edify—to build up others in their Christian faith and life.

2. Preachers, teachers, and worship leaders need to share Paul's concern that the language they use in preaching, teaching, or leading worship communicates the Gospel effectively and efficiently. Preaching, teaching, and worship are too important to simply fill in time or make noise—even impressive, high-sounding noise.

3. Paul lists a variety of elements in the public worship services of the Corinthian church. Some of these elements may be different from parts of the service today (revelations, tongues, and the interpretation of tongues). Today, God's revelation comes through His Word. So in our worship, Scripture is interpreted in the language of the people, not in a foreign tongue. Nevertheless, the principle Paul states remains a determining principle for anyone involved in planning services of worship: everything must be done for the strengthening of the church.

4. Paul's principle is that worship is to glorify God by strengthening the people's faith in Jesus Christ. Obviously, people will not be strengthened if the Gospel is not proclaimed so that they can understand it.

5. The basic principles Paul wrote about are as applicable today as in Paul's own day since they are grounded in the structure of creation itself and are supported by the principle of Christian love. Some of the customs referred to in the Bible (such as head coverings in **11:2–16**) are no longer applicable to us today, even as they were not universally applicable in their own day. But the principles that lie behind such customs (the relationship between men and women built into the structure of God's creation) apply as well today as ever.

Closing

Sing or speak together the closing hymn. Ask participants for prayer concerns or requests. Pray or have a volunteer pray for those things identified by the participants.

Lesson 14

Hope in the Resurrection (1 Corinthians 15–16)

Theme Verse

Invite a volunteer to read the theme verse for this lesson.

Goal

Read aloud the goal statement. Point out that the goal will briefly describe the direction the lesson will take.

What's Going On Here?

Read aloud or have a volunteer read aloud this introductory section.

Searching the Scriptures

Read aloud or have volunteers read aloud the suggested portions of Scripture before discussing the questions.

Witness Bearers of the Resurrection (1 Corinthians 15:1–11)

1. The Gospel recounted in **verses 3–5** focuses on Christ's death "for our sins" and on His resurrection. Paul not only asserts that Christ rose from the dead, but he marshals eyewitnesses whose testimony proves that Christ rose.

2. Christ's resurrection was a historical event, involving His physical body, in our real world. It was, therefore, something that could be seen by eyewitnesses. Paul appealed to the testimony of those eyewitnesses. While we today do not have the advantage of being able to interview these eyewitnesses, we nevertheless have their testimony recorded in Scripture. Note also that Paul's readers could have verified the facts of Christ's resurrection with any or all of those Paul mentions as still living. Paul himself was obviously confident of what their testimony would be.

3. Grace is the unmerited favor and the forgiving love of God. Paul never claimed to deserve the place God had given him. In fact, Paul declared that he, of all people, was least deserving. Whatever Paul accomplished for the Lord he credited to God's power and not to his own effort.

Christ Has Conquered Death (1 Corinthians 15:12–34)

1. Accept reasonable answers drawn from the text. These may include the truth that if the dead are not raised, then Christ was not raised either. If that were true, then to proclaim the Gospel is useless and a lie, our faith is futile, we are still in our sins, those who died are lost, and all those who have put their hope in Christ are to be pitied.

2. Christ is now reigning, or ruling, over His church through the Gospel.

3. While we do not understand what Paul meant by the reference to being baptized for the dead, we know that it cannot mean that someone who died without believing in Christ will be saved anyway if a believer is baptized on that person's behalf. Scripture clearly teaches that a personal faith relationship is necessary for salvation. It also teaches that after death comes the judgment—not another opportunity to be saved, either by our own doing or by what someone else does on our behalf. We may guess at what Paul meant, but it seems unlikely that we will know.

Rising with Glorified Bodies (1 Corinthians 15:35–58)

1. Paul uses three analogies: **verses 36–38,** plants and seeds; **verse 39,** the many varieties of living things; **verses 40–41,** heavenly bodies (e.g., sun, moon) contrasted with the earth.

2. Our perishable, mortal bodies will be changed and become imperishable and immortal. The change will take place when Christ returns. It will be instantaneous and will take place simultaneously in all believers. Those who are still living when Christ returns will find their bodies instantly changed. Those in the grave on that day will be raised from death and changed as they rise.

3. We Christians may stand firm and give ourselves fully to the Lord's work because Christ has risen from death and has overcome the power of Satan and sin. The Lord now lives to strengthen and encourage us in our daily struggles and service.

Christian Giving (1 Corinthians 16:1–24)

1. God's people **(v. 1)** were the poor among the saints in Jerusalem **(Romans 15:26).** They may have been poor because of the famine predicted by Agabus **(Acts 11:28),** which took place in A.D. 44 or 46, or due to persecution **(Acts 9:1).**

2. Paul encourages the congregation to be on guard, stand firm in the

faith, be courageous, be strong, and do everything in love.

3. The congregation should submit in the sense of following their leadership and giving them respect, appreciation, and cooperation.

The Word for Us

1. Have participants share how the Gospel has produced faith and faith-filled living in their lives. This is not bragging, but rather it is glorifying God for the work He has done in them through the Gospel.

2. If Christ had not been raised, then our faith is useless and we are still in our sins.

3. From the three examples to which Paul refers we learn our resurrected bodies will emerge from our present body, but those resurrection bodies will be much greater and more beautiful, just as a mature plant is greater and more beautiful than the seemingly dead seed from which it sprang.

4. Paul instructed the Corinthians to set aside an offering each week. This offering was to be in proportion to the giver's income. This principle of regular, proportionate giving is as applicable to us today as it was to the Corinthians.

Closing

Sing or speak together the closing hymn. Ask participants for prayer concerns or requests. Pray or have a volunteer pray for those things identified by the participants.